Best Practice Guide

for Customer Service Professionals

Customer 1st International

United Kingdom

Best Practice Guide for Customer Service Professionals 2nd Edition

Published by Customer 1st International Ltd 2006

ISBN: 0-9548744-1-2

Published in the UK 2006 by
Customer 1st International Ltd
Bramblewood House
Longbridge Deverill
Wiltshire BA12 7DS
United Kingdom

Printed and bound in the UK by
Solent Design Studio Ltd
Bishop's Waltham
Southampton
Hampshire SO32 1BH
United Kingdom

Illustrations by Anne-Marie Sonneveld

Contents

1

8   Laws and codes of practice   155

9   The you factor   179

3

Introduction

The aims and objectives of this Best Practice Guide

The Best Practice Guide for Customer Service Professionals is for all those who deal with customers. Working effectively with customers demands more than customer care. Today's customers want to deal with real professionals, representing organisations that meet their high expectations. Your customers may be internal (within your organisation) or external (outside your organisation). The skills needed are very similar, and the Best Practice Guide will help you to focus on improving the skills that you need in your work.

The Best Practice Guide covers all the knowledge and skills needed to deliver excellent customer service. It has been based on the UK's National Occupational Standards for Customer Service (released in 2006). The Guide delivers all the concepts, knowledge and understanding through simple explanations and examples. It then enables you to improve your skills by carrying out relevant, work-based activities involving your own customers.

The importance of the customer service professional

You individually play a key part in the success of your organisation. As a customer service professional you can make the difference for the customer. Your actions can turn new or even unhappy customers into loyal ambassadors for your organisation. Your skills and knowledge can provide customers with exactly what they are looking for. This will encourage them to return to your organisation over and over again – and this in turn can bring financial success.

TOP TIP

Customer service is all about YOU ...

... your skills, your knowledge, your attitude, your team working and your communications

4

Your organisation has ambitious aims and objectives. But without you and your fellow professionals working well as a customer service team, those plans cannot be realised. So as you progress through this improvement programme, remember that it is all about you. You can develop your skills in dealing with customers to the highest possible level. You can not only achieve success on behalf of your organisation, but you can also gain yourself – through job satisfaction, reward and recognition.

Learning outcomes

The learning outcomes for this Best Practice Guide describe what you will be able to do after successfully completing all the modules. Each module's learning outcomes are shown below.

5

Module 1	Basic concepts of customer service

When you have successfully read through all the explanations and completed all the activities in this module you will be able to:

- Demonstrate an understanding of the basic concepts of customer service

- Understand the importance to customers and of receiving excellent customer service

- Understand how an organisation's reputation can depend upon the delivery of excellent customer service

- Distinguish between different levels of customer service

- Demonstrate an understanding of how the service offer can be enhanced by added service value

- Explain a range of methods of measuring customer service

- Identify moments of truth in a customer service context

Module 2	Developing relationships with your customers

When you have successfully read through all the explanations and completed all the activities in this module you will be able to:

- Recognise and distinguish between internal and external customers

- Understand the benefits and importance of customer loyalty

- Identify the components of an effective customer service process

Module 3   Customer service in different organisations

When you have successfully read through all the explanations and completed all the activities in this module you will be able to:

- Explain why customer service is important to different types of organisation

- Explain how customer service differs in different types of organisation

- Recognise how the service offer tends to vary for different types of organisations

Module 4   Match features and benefits

When you have successfully read through all the explanations and completed all the activities in this module you will be able to:

- Demonstrate an understanding of features and benefits of products and services that affect the delivery of customer service

- Identify customer preferences and match them to available options

- Recognise how organisations can set product and service standards

- Demonstrate an understanding of equality and diversity issues for an organisation

- Demonstrate an understanding of how to promote additional services or products to customers

- Identify an unique selling point for a product or service

Module 5   Communicate effectively

When you have successfully read through all the explanations and completed all the activities in this module you will be able to:

- Describe the importance of effective communication in the delivery of customer service

- Choose the most appropriate communication method to suit a specific customer service situation

- Recognise the value of effective verbal and non-verbal communication skills in customer service transactions

- Choose behaviour that is appropriate to a specific customer service situation

- Understand the benefits, features and methods of using information and communications technology (ICT) in order to deliver effective customer service

Module 6   Deliver service excellence through teamwork

When you have successfully read through all the explanations and completed all the activities in this module you will be able to:

- Demonstrate an understanding of effective methods of team working in the delivery of customer service

- Identify examples of working in partnership with other organisations

Module 7   Systems for delivering service excellence

When you have successfully read through all the explanations and completed all the activities in this module you will be able to:

- Explain the importance of systems and procedures supporting consistent delivery of customer service

- Demonstrate an understanding that systems should be focused on customers

- Identify customer preferences and match them to available options

- Understand the meaning and benefits of product and service innovation

- Explain how organisations can benefit from customer feedback, both positive and negative

- Describe a systematic approach to service recovery

- Identify effective ways of resolving customers' problems

- Deal effectively with difficult customers and difficult customer service situations

- Understand the importance of using ICT to support systems and customers

Module 8   Laws and codes of practice

When you have successfully read through all the explanations and completed all the activities in this module you will be able to:

- Understand the main aspects of customer service that are affected by legislation, regulation and sector codes of practice

- Recognise the main regulatory and legal restrictions on what you can and cannot do in all aspects of your work with customers

7

Module 9   The you factor

When you have successfully read through all the explanations and completed all the activities in this module you will be able to:

- Identify the skills of emotional intelligence that are relevant to customer service

- Demonstrate an understanding of the effects of submissive, assertive and aggressive behaviours on others

- Understand how personal attitude, health and emotional state affect your ability to deliver excellent customer service

- Plan and carry out activities that are needed for your own professional development

This Best Practice Guide covers the knowledge and skills required by the U.K.'s Level 2 National Occupational Standards for Customer Service. After module 9 you will find an S/NVQ knowledge matrix that maps the knowledge requirements of the National Occupational Standards (NOS) to this Best Practice Guide. This shows you, section by section, where you cover the knowledge requirements of the Level 2 NOS for Customer Service.

Introducing the knowledge and skills that you need

As a professional you will need specific knowledge and skills. These take time, effort and motivation to develop. The Best Practice Guide will show you how to develop that set of skills and knowledge. This may be done either in your job role or within a learning programme.

We hope you find the Best Practice Guide informative and fun.   For someone new to customer service all the concepts, guide-lines and activities will prepare you to operate as a true professional. If you are already experienced in dealing with customers you will discover new ideas and find ways of improving your expertise. Each module introduces you to customer service knowledge and skills. There are examples and illustrations to help you relate the knowledge and skills to your own experience and job role.

The activities and learning log

You should complete the activities as you go through each module of the Best Practice Guide. They will help you to consolidate your learning. They allow you to apply what you learn to your own organisation, or to one that you are familiar with.

If at the moment you are not employed, or in a position where you do not deal directly with customers, do not worry – you can still carry out the activities by applying them to organisations that you deal with in your everyday life.

To get you started, complete the following activity.

Activity

Your personal objectives for the Best Practice Guide

To start with, think about what you hope to get out of this development programme. Where in your customer service role do you need to improve your own understanding and skills? Decide on your personal objectives which will enable you to improve your performance as a customer service professional. Write in the space below up to five personal objectives for your development programme.

1	
2	
3	
4	
5	

9

Use the learning log for each module. This will help you to reflect on your learning. It will encourage you to plan changes and improvements – and to put them into place. Here is a your first learning log.

Your learning log

This is not simply a learning programme. It is important that you make real changes and improvements to the way you work. Use the learning log to record what you have learned and the actions that you plan to take. Add items to your learning log. When you get to the end of the programme you will need to refine these items to produce a clear action plan.

What I have learned
1
2
3
4
5

Actions planned	Target date
1	
2	
3	
4	
5	

Confirming your learning

The Best Practice Guide for Customer Service Professionals will help you to track your own progress and improvements. Each module ends with a multichoice self-assessment consisting of five questions. Each self-assessment checks the progress you have made with your learning programme. You should carry out the self-assessment once you have finished going through the module, including all the activities. You will find the answers to the self-assessments towards the end of this Best Practice Guide.

Moving on to further learning

Once you have completed this Best Practice Guide you may want to achieve one of the following vocational qualifications:

- The Level 2 Certificate in Customer Service - this is also known as the Level 2 Technical Certificate in Customer Service
- The Level 2 National Vocational Qualification (NVQ) or Scottish Vocational Qualification (SVQ) in Customer Service - this assesses how you apply your knowledge and skills in the workplace

To take your learning even further you may consider a qualification for supervisors or junior managers in customer service:

- The Level 3 Certificate in Customer Service - this assesses your knowledge and skills as a supervisor or team leader, and is also known as the Level 3 Technical Certificate in Customer Service
- The Level 3 National Vocational Qualification (NVQ) or Scottish Vocational Qualification (SVQ) in Customer Service - this assesses how you apply your knowledge and skills in the workplace as a supervisor or team leader

11

Module 1: Basic concepts of customer service

Module introduction

Welcome to Module 1 of the Best Practice Guide for Customer Service Professionals. In this module we look at the basic concepts of customer service, what our customers expect, and standards of customer service.

1.1 Learning outcomes

When you have successfully read through all the explanations and completed all the activities in this module you will be able to:

- Demonstrate an understanding of the basic concepts of customer service
- Understand the importance to customers and of receiving excellent customer service
- Understand how an organisation's reputation can depend upon the delivery of excellent customer service
- Distinguish between different levels of customer service
- Demonstrate an understanding of how the service offer can be enhanced by added service value
- Explain a range of methods of measuring customer service
- Identify moments of truth in a customer service context

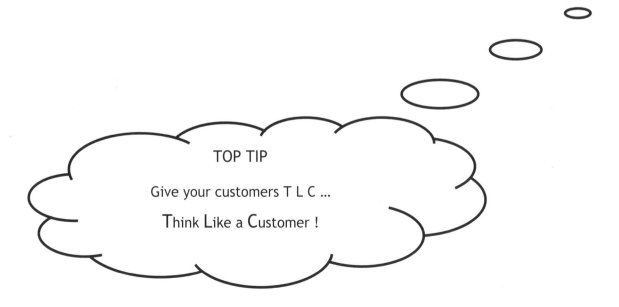

TOP TIP

Give your customers T L C ...

Think Like a Customer !

1.2 What is customer service?

Let us start off with some ideas on what we actually mean by customer service.

What is customer service?
Think about the customer service that you provide to your customers. In your own words, write down what you think customer service means. If you want to, refer to the organisation you work for, or one that you are familiar with.

13

Definition	Customer service is the sum total of what an organisation does to meet customer expectations and produce customer satisfaction.
Customer service	

Types of customer service

There are different types of customer service delivered at different stages. We can identify customer service delivered before the sale of the product or service, during the sale, and after the sale. Let us look at some examples.

Customer service in a restaurant	
Customer service before sale	Welcoming the customer into the restaurant
Customer service during sale	Serving the food in a friendly and efficient manner
Customer service after sale	Asking the customer if everything was satisfactory
Customer service in a car dealership	
Customer service before sale	Providing information and a test drive
Customer service during sale	Handling the finance for the customer's purchase of a new car
Customer service after sale	Dealing with after sales servicing in a friendly and efficient manner
Customer service in a hotel	
Customer service before sale	Confirming the availability of rooms for specific dates
Customer service during sale	Responding to a customer's request to change to a quieter room
Customer service after sale	Returning customers' belongings that were left in the room in error

To do the same for your own organisation, complete the next activity.

Activity

Customer service in my own organisation	
Give an example of customer service at each of the three stages.	
Customer service before sale	
Customer service during sale	
Customer service after sale	

1.3 Customer satisfaction

You have probably heard of the term customer satisfaction. Here is a definition.

Definition	Customer satisfaction is the feeling that a customer gets when he or she is happy with the customer service that has been provided.
Customer satisfaction	

A satisfied customer is one who has received the level of service he or she expected; nothing went wrong and the customer went away reasonably "happy". But is this enough? What if the customer tries another competing business to yours, and is not merely satisfied, but delighted? Try to delight your customers by giving them more than they expected.   Customers are very demanding, and if your organisation cannot delight them they will probably go to another.

One positive step you can make in your organisation is to measure the level of customer satisfaction. You need to get feedback from your customers to find out what they think of your level of service. You can get feedback from your customers by:

- asking them questions
- listening to them
- encouraging them to complete customer satisfaction questionnaires
- dealing with their suggestions for improvements
- handling their complaints

You might think of the different levels of customer satisfaction as (for example):

- delighted
- satisfied
- disappointed
- unsatisfied

On the other hand you might measure customer satisfaction by a score (out of ten, say) by analysing customer satisfaction questionnaires. However you do it, it is vital that you and your organisation know how satisfied your customers are, and always try to "go the extra mile" to delight your customers.

15

Listening to your customer

Be aware that customers are changing. They expect more than they used to, especially in terms of the service they receive. Study and then discuss with your colleagues the following statistics.

Customer satisfaction facts and figures

Here are some facts and figures about customer satisfaction in the UK.

Customer service

- Customer satisfaction is declining, not improving
  (ABA Research Ltd and Surrey University, 2003)

- 60% of customers think customer service in the UK is getting worse, while 40% think it is not improving
  (ABA Research Ltd and Surrey University, 2003)

- 69% of customers would be willing to pay up to 20% more for exceptional customer service
  (Hicks, NCCS 2006)

- 58% of customers say companies are putting profit before consumers and 42% say companies do not encourage complaints.
  (Hicks, 2006)

1.4 Customer expectations

You cannot plan properly to satisfy or delight your customers until you know something about their expectations. To understand the expectations of the customer, try to see it from the customer's point of view.

Remember that customers are individuals. Each one has a set of expectations of the service that you will provide. It is a vital part of your job to try to live up to and exceed those expectations. To help you do that, think like a customer.

Your organisation could "see it from the customer's point of view" on a regular basis. For example some organisations (such as shops, restaurants and hotels) use mystery shoppers to experience the level of service first hand. The mystery shopper goes into the organisation unannounced and checks the levels of service given against certain criteria. Feedback is then given to the staff and/or managers in order to identify where improvements can be made.

17

Activity

Customer expectations

Think of an example of poor customer service that you have experienced personally. In that organisation the customer service did not meet your expectations. Describe what went wrong, then list the things that would need to improve so that the service would meet your expectations.

Quote from ...	"I think in here they all know we offer help and a happy cheery smiling face at the check-out or at the customer service or the petrol station. That is what they expect, and that is what they get." (Johnston, 2003)
Tesco	

Definition	Customer expectations are what people think should happen and how they think they should be treated when asking for or receiving customer service.
Customer expectations	

Customer expectations can be complex. Think about how your customers' expectations are formed. Why do customers expect what they do of your products and services? Try to see things from the customer's point of view in the next activity.

"70 % is about fixing the person, 30 % is about fixing the car"

Your expectations as a customer

Pick a commercially available product or service that you buy. Choose one which has other competing products/services in the marketplace.

Name of the product /service	

How your expectations are formed

What do you look for in this product/service?	
Why do you choose to buy it from this particular business?	
How do you know what to expect from the product/service?	
Describe briefly your expectations as a customer	
How do the competing products/services compare to the one you choose?	
What ideas do you get from your family, friends or colleagues about the product/service?	
Describe briefly any advertisements, brochures, websites or other media that inform you about this product	

Price and value

How does the price compare to its competitors?	
How does the value for money compare to its competitors?	

19

From the last activity you have seen the difference between good and poor customer service. Now we need to think about the levels of customer service that we can provide. It is easy to say that we should provide excellence, but what does "excellent customer service" actually mean? Complete the next activity to find out.

Activity

What is excellent customer service?

Think about the level of customer service that your organisation provides. How good is it? Here are some ideas of what excellent customer service means:

- *Meeting customers' needs*
- *Exceeding peoples' expectations*
- *Delighting the customer*
- *Making a good first impression*
- *Going the extra mile for the customer*
- *Providing a first class product and service*

All of these ideas are good ideas. But for you in your organisation it is vital that you discover what your customers expect, and then find ways of meeting and exceeding those expectations.

Now be specific about your own organisation, or one that you are familiar with. What would excellent customer service look like to one of your customers? Write down three ways of providing excellent service to your customers.

1	
2	
3	

Views of service excellence

Here are some quotes from people who work for organisations that have been recognised for the high level of customer service that they provide. Employees were asked what they thought excellent customer service means. The quotes show how customer service professionals think. (All quotes from Johnston, 2003).

Quotes from First Direct employees:

- Good service means that calls get answered promptly; customers get their issues dealt with on one call wherever possible. They get an efficient service, they can trust us to carry out their instructions as and when they require them

- By being there in the first place and picking up the calls quicker than any other organisation

Quotes from Shangri-La Hotels employees:

- When I meet them, I give them smiles. I greet them with friendliness, with sincerity, and hospitality. I give them a warm welcome

- Customers expect good and simple services without fussiness

- If a customer cried Wow!!!, after his or her first time tasting of my food, it would be the best. It was beyond his or her expectation. Food should always look tempting and smell great

- When we give them more than they asked for, this will impress them

Quotes from Tesco employees:

- The food looks good, the way that it is set out. The freshness is obvious

- Smile and be friendly towards the customers

- Generally they are dealt with straightaway

- Always give the best service possible

- Well, I always try to be pleasant. I always try to be as helpful as I possibly can

23

But why should we provide excellent customer service? Perhaps we should just do the minimum. No! If you and your organisation do not excel in customer service, the customers will go elsewhere.

Give the customer a warm welcome

1.6 Customer service transactions

Definition	A customer service transaction is a single exchange of information, product or service between a customer and a service deliverer.
Customer service transaction	

Your customers link up with you through customer transactions. Your organisation carries out many different transactions with customers. During an individual transaction, the customer may do, for example, one of the following:

- Request information from you
- Buy a service or product
- Make an agreement with you
- Log a complaint
- Book an appointment

- Return an item for repair

Your customers form their opinions of you and your organisation during these customer service transactions. They may get opinions from elsewhere, such as from friends, colleagues and relatives who have dealt with you, but they will make their judgments mainly on the basis of these transactions. Therefore, you have to get these transactions right! The transaction should be for the customer an easy, pleasant and positive experience. Aim to provide excellent service during every single transaction.

1.7 The service offer and added service value

The actual services that a customer is offered when he or she considers a purchase varies from one product to another. They also vary from one organisation to another.

25

The service offered by a luxury, five-star hotel is considerably more than that offered by a basic bed & breakfast business. The customer takes his or her choice. In the same way, a customer expects a much higher level of service at a high-class restaurant than from a burger bar!

Definition	A service offer defines the extent and limits of the customer service that an organisation is offering.
Service Offer	

Price and the service offer

The higher the price of the basic product or service being purchased, the greater the service offer tends to be. This is not always the case though. For example, if you buy an inexpensive small car you expect more or less the same level of service as if you had bought an expensive, luxury car. In general though a higher price tends to mean that the organisation can afford to provide extra services.

Look at similar products offered by different organisations. As an example, in the UK, everyone pays towards the running of the National Health Service through National Insurance contributions and taxes. When you become ill and have to go to hospital for treatment you can choose to go to an NHS hospital. Or, if you can afford it, you may choose a private hospital. This costs more. You pay the hospital fees or medical insurance in addition to the NI contributions and taxes. However, you will expect to receive a better level of service. The service offer is greater because of the higher price of the product.

Other organisations and the service offer

Your organisation might choose to improve the service offer in order to win more business (if it is in competition with other organisations). For instance Starbucks, the global coffee shop, provides a unique service offer by providing more comfortable surroundings in an atmosphere that encourages customers to stay longer. They don't just drink coffee; they enjoy a much wider "experience". Starbucks made this service offer a success.

26

Starbucks shops in the United States also provide wireless internet connections. Customers with a laptop computer equipped with a suitable "Wifi" wireless connection can connect up to the internet to check their emails and surf the web. This service innovation extended the Starbucks' service offer.

TOP TIP

Don't be afraid of making suggestions to your manager – you are the one who knows best what the problems and solutions are!

Now complete the next activity.

Extend the service offer

Choose three well-known organisations. For each one, think of one way of extending the service offer, which may benefit the business.

Name of organisation	How the service offer could be extended

Now do the same for your own organisation

Name of organisation	How the service offer could be extended

Another way of ensuring that a not-for-profit organisation is performing well is to look at the added service value that it provides to its customers. Look at this definition of added service value.

Definition	Added service value is the extra, over and above the basic product or service provided, that an organisation offers to its customers. This added service value represents extra service benefits that can truly delight the customers and keep them loyal.
Added service value	

Added service value

1.8 Benchmarking

Whatever an organisation's aims are, customer service is very important to achieving them. Customer service can enhance reputation and give added service value. Benchmarking should be used to ensure that the level of customer service is as high as possible.

Definition	Performance Benchmarking is the process of trying to reach target levels of performance that are achieved by the best organisations. The organisations could be in the same sector, or another sector.
Performance Benchmarking	

Benchmarking is good for you and good for your customers. If you benchmark your levels of customer service against other organisations (or other sectors, or even other countries) you will be aware of the best practice. You will be inspired to copy elements of that best practice to your own situation. Benchmarking is not simply reaching the same standard that others have reached. It is really about raising the level of service that you provide to the best possible. If you can do that then you will delight your customers and establish a reputation for excellence.

Benchmark against the best organisation that you know of. Think of businesses that are well known for their excellent customer service. Now try to transfer that excellence to your own organisation. This is how to excel at customer service – be different and innovative. Think of ways of delighting your customers that no-one else has thought of.

Now complete the next activity.

Activity

Case Study : Performance benchmarking

Look at this sample case study from the care sector. Read the case study and write your answers in the spaces provided.

Pro-Care Homes

Pro-Care is an organisation that runs 15 care homes for elderly people. It is a not-for-profit organisation. It has charitable status. It is funded by a number of charities, plus some direct donations from the public.

Chrissie Clarke is the Operations Manager for Pro-Care, and she works at Head Office. She oversees the management of each of the 15 care homes, making sure they provide the best possible level of service to the customers. Chrissie uses performance benchmarking to set targets for the care home managers. She uses information provided by researchers in the care sector, who provide statistics on a range of service levels in UK care homes. She uses the service levels of the country's best care homes as performance benchmarks. In this way she knows that, if Pro-Care homes achieve their targets they will be some of the best homes in the whole country.

One service that she wants to improve is how the staff in the homes respond to requests from the relatives of the elderly patients. Chrissie has set the following targets for the year ahead. Care home managers must do whatever is needed to try to meet these targets.

29

Performance aim	Benchmark	Current Pro-Care figure	Pro-Care target
1 To inform relatives quickly of any change in the patient's condition	3 hours	7.5 hours	3 hours
2 To increase the maximum visiting hours per week	20 hours	8 hours	15 hours
3 To reduce the average time to respond to a telephone message	45 minutes	2.5 hours	1 hour

Questions	Your answers
What might the Pro-Care home managers need to do to achieve Target 1?	
If the homes achieve Target 2, what will the customers think of this?	
What problems might the managers and staff come across in trying to achieve Target 3?	
Do you think all targets can be measured as numbers, like the ones above? If not, what other kinds of targets can be set?	
How could Chrissie find out the general level of customer satisfaction with each of the Pro-Care homes?	

30

1.9 Measuring service standards

To benchmark against others you need to measure your own performance. Think of ways of doing that. You may have questionnaires or other methods of getting feedback. Here are some ideas on how to use service standards:

- Use customer satisfaction questionnaires
- Analyse your questionnaires – and do something with the results. Action plan your improvements, so that your customer feedback is used to make a difference
- Keep track of your performance (that is your own and your team's performance)

- Publish the results of your performance measurement - make easy to understand graphs and put them up on notice boards - let everyone know how you are doing and how you can improve
- Show your results to your customers - they are interested in how you are doing
- Show your results to your other stakeholders - managers, shareholders, directors, suppliers, and everyone else who is interested in the success of your organisation
- Track improvements over time - put up on the notice board a graph showing progress against planned improvements

1.10 Moments of truth

In dealings with customers there are moments of truth. Here is a definition:

| Definition

Moment of Truth	A moment of truth is a critically important point in time when a customer forms an opinion about the organisation's level of service. At a moment of truth the customer will either decide to stay loyal to the organisation, or go elsewhere, perhaps to a competitor.

Here are some examples of moments of truth. Study them before you tackle the activity that follows.

Activity

Moments of truth	
Organisation	A moment of truth
A package holiday company	The point when the customer logs into the company's website. The potential customer will move onto another site unless this one seems easy to use.
A superstore	The point when the shopper asks an assistant for help in finding a product. The assistant needs good product knowledge - if not, the moment of truth is not a good one!

In the next activity you get the chance to think about the moments of truth that you have experienced as a customer.

Moments of truth for you as a customer

Remember a situation when you were a customer. Perhaps it was in a restaurant, a public house or hotel. Think of three moments of truth that made a big impression on your view of the organisation's customer service. (They could be positive or negative).

1	
2	
3	

You understand what moments of truth are. They can be different for every person and every organisation. What you can be sure of, though, is that the customers of your organisation do have their own moments of truth. In the next activity you will be able to identify some moments of truth in your own organisation, or one that you are familiar with.

32

Moments of truth in your organisation

Now find three moments of truth for your own organisation. Briefly explain each one.

My organisation	3 moments of truth	
	1	
	2	
	3	

33

1.11 Self-assessment

Module 1 Self-assessment

In each case tick the answer that best fits the question.

1	Customer satisfaction is:	Smiling at the customer	A	☐
		The feeling of being happy with the service provided	B	☐
		Filling in the satisfaction questionnaire	C	☐
2	You can get feedback from your customers by:	Showing them the new brochure	A	☐
		Handling their complaints	B	☐
		Taking their payment	C	☐
3	Mystery shoppers:	Check service given against certain criteria	A	☐
		Are all buyers of products	B	☐
		Are customers who buy on impulse	C	☐
4	A good way of understanding what customers expect is to:	Tell them all about your products and services	A	☐
		Read the newspapers	B	☐
		Put yourself in the customer's shoes	C	☐
5	Moments of truth are when:	The manager carries out your appraisal	A	☐
		Customers form an opinion about your level of service	B	☐
		The company has financial problems	C	☐

34

1.12 Learning log

Now complete your learning log.

Activity

Learning log for Module 1

Add items to your learning log. When you get to the end of the programme you will need to refine these items to produce a clear action plan.

What I have learned
1
2
3
4
5

Actions planned	Target date
1	
2	
3	
4	
5	

35

Module summary

- Well done – in this module you have learned about the basic meanings and concepts of customer service. You have identified what "customer service" means, and you have discovered what customers expect in a variety of organisations. Moments of truth are important because they help customers to judge your organisation. There is a clear difference between good and poor customer service and you have seen some examples of excellent service from very successful organisations. Benchmarking is used to learn best practice from, or share it with other organisations. These might be similar organisations – or very different ones – to your own.

Module 2: Developing relationships with your customers

Module introduction

Welcome to Module 2 of the Best Practice Guide for Customer Service Professionals. In this module we look the relationships that we have with our customers. You will discover the essential components that need to be in place for an organisation to deliver excellent service. We also find out how to keep customers loyal, and the benefits that customer loyalty brings.

2.1 Learning outcomes

When you have successfully read through all the explanations and completed all the activities in this module you will be able to:

- Recognise and distinguish between internal and external customers
- Understand the benefits and importance of customer loyalty
- Identify the components of an effective customer service process

2.2 Internal customers and external customers

You deal with different types of customers. One distinction is between internal customers and external customers.

Definition	Internal customers are people from the same organisation as the service provider. They are treated as a customer so that they in turn can provide better customer service to external customers.
Internal customers	

You should regard all the people you work with as customers, because your job is to provide them with a service. In fact, many of the organisations with the best customer service have achieved their high standards through getting the service right for internal customers first of all.

Definition	An external customer is a customer who accesses your product or service from outside your organisation.
External customers	

Again, it is essential that you give external customers the best possible level of service. The next activity will help you to be clear about internal and external customers.

Activity

Internal and external customers

Work out who are your internal and external customers. Base this activity on your own organisation, or one that you know well.

Internal customers	External customers
List 3 internal customers who you have dealt with in the past week.	*List 3 external customers who you have dealt with in the past week.*
1	1
2	2
3	3

2.3 Customer relationships

You and your organisation deal with many customers over the days, weeks, months and years. All these customers are individuals. Each has their own expectations. Some customers will come back to your organisation time after time. Others may only stay with you for one purchase or transaction.

One of your aims must be to keep your customers for as long as possible. Apart from any other factor, it is expensive to lose customers. Your business has to spend money and resources in gaining new customers, which is far more difficult than keeping your existing ones.

Definition	A customer relationship forms as the result of a number of individual customer service transactions.
Customer relationship	

The best customer relationship is a long-lasting one. A prime reason for you to give excellent customer service is that it will tend to keep your customers loyal – it will provide your organisation with more long-term customer relationships.

By the way, giving excellent service does not just keep your existing customers for longer – it also means that those loyal customers will tell their friends, relatives and colleagues about you, and you will gain new customers without spending any extra resources on advertising or promotion. Word of mouth is the best possible way of spreading the word about your organisation.

39

Quote from ...	"We will demonstrate honesty and care in all our relationships." (Johnston, 2003)
Shangri-La	

2.4 The components of the customer service process

To deliver excellent customer service your organisation must make sure that everything is in place for the customers.

Organisational vision and strategy

If this is present the senior management of the organisation has realised that customer service is vitally important to the success of the organisation. Customer service should be included in the vision and/or mission statement of the organisation. Everyone should understand the importance of customers in the organisation's plans.

involve your colleagues, and do you know if they are available? Do you know how to use the correct procedure? A lot of this depends upon your own particular organisation and the particular product or service it provides.

Deliver

When you deliver customer service you need to get it right every time. Remember about moments of truth. For a customer this could be your one opportunity to get it right. If you have the right skills, information and support you can delight your customer and begin to build a long term customer relationship.

Follow-up

Always follow up the delivery of customer service. You need to find out what went well and what can be improved. The next activity is to get you thinking about feedback and improvements to the service you provide. Think about how you follow up your service delivery.

Follow-up your service delivery

Answer the questions below about how your own organisation follows up its service delivery.

1. Do you use questionnaires and/or mystery shoppers?

2. How effective is the follow up after service delivery?

3. What do you do with results?

4. Can you say what will happen when a number of customers complain about a particular customer service transaction? Who investigates?

5. Who takes action to re-design the service delivery procedure?

6. Who re-trains the staff involved?

43

2.5 Customer Loyalty

In order to build and keep customer loyalty the type of service provided can depend upon the type of organisation. Let us look at customer loyalty first of all.

Definition	Some customers tend to return to the same service deliverer and this is customer loyalty. Customers will stay loyal if the organisation "delivers the promise."
Customer Loyalty	

Achieving and maintaining a reputation for excellence

What your customers think of the services and products that your business offers will determine whether they will stay loyal or go elsewhere. If they go elsewhere it will be to a competitor, which is not good for your business. The service you provide to your customers can make a big difference to the financial success of the business. So how do you keep the customers loyal?

Repeat business through customer loyalty

Your existing customers are easiest to keep. They know you and your organisation. They trust you. They know you provide the products and services they want. If you are losing customers you must be doing something wrong, because otherwise customers would rather stay with you. Today's customers will "shop around". They will not stay loyal without a good reason. They are generally smart enough to seek out the best products and services available.

How to lose customers

You and your organisation cannot afford to lose existing customers. It is too expensive and time consuming to find new ones. It costs around five times as much to recruit a new customer as it does to keep an existing one. So make sure your organisation is maximising its repeat business through keeping customers loyal. If this is not happening, tell your manager and talk to your colleagues about it.

Unfortunately, there are many ways to lose customers! Here are just a few of them:

- Giving poor service
- Having complicated processes for customers
- Products not meeting customers' expectations

- Service not meeting customers' expectations
- Not being interested in customers
- Not listening to customers
- Dealing with a customer complaint or problem poorly or slowly
- Competitors having better service
- Competitors having better products
- Competitors having lower prices
- Not making customers feel special or valued

If your organisation gets these things wrong you will certainly lose some of the customers you have. Even worse is the damage that can be done to your organisation's reputation. If its reputation is damaged it will be even more difficult to find new customers.

45

New business through customer loyalty

You can even get new business through keeping your existing customers loyal. In fact this is the best way to get new business. This is because it is not only your existing customers who you want to keep loyal. It is their friends and relatives as well. Everyone likes to tell their friends, relatives and colleagues about businesses that provide good value and good service. If you discover a business that is really exceptional, offering startling levels of service, you are just bursting to tell people about it! This sort of promotion is often more effective than expensive marketing campaigns. This method of gaining new business is known as referrals. Existing customers will also buy new products and services if they are delighted with the first products and services they bought.

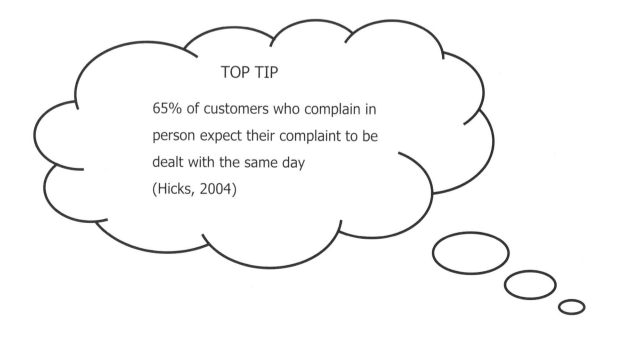

TOP TIP

65% of customers who complain in person expect their complaint to be dealt with the same day (Hicks, 2004)

Customer loyalty leads to lower costs and stable finances

There are other important benefits to your organisation of keeping a big base of loyal customers. Not only will the organisation need to spend less on marketing. (Marketing includes selling and promoting your products and services). Look at the diagram below. It shows what you need to achieve loyal customers, and some of the benefits that loyal customers can bring.

46

Having a base of loyal customers provides a stable cash flow for the organisation. This is good for the organisation and therefore for you. After all, for most businesses the cash from the customers pays the employees' wages. Even for a not-for-profit organisation, stable finances are good news for the employees.

2.6   Benefits of customer service

Let us be clear about exactly why customer service is so important. If you and your organisation can get the service you provide to your customers right, then you will see specific benefits.

Activity

Benefits of customer service

Write in the table below the benefits of effective customer service to the customer, organisation and employee. Try to think of at least 3 benefits for each.

Benefits to the customer:

1	
2	
3	
4	

Benefits to the organisation:

1	
2	
3	
4	

Benefits to the employee:

1	
2	
3	
4	

47

2.7 Self-assessment

Module 2 Self-assessment

In each case tick the answer that best fits the question.

1	Internal customers should be treated	As well as external customers	A	☐
		Differently from external customers	B	☐
		Better than external customers	C	☐
2	A reason for keeping customers loyal is that:	They are much more friendly	A	☐
		It is expensive to lose them	B	☐
		They will make bigger purchases	C	☐
3	The best customer relationships are:	Quick ones	A	☐
		Informal ones	B	☐
		Long-lasting ones	C	☐
4	The organisation's structure should:	Be very strong	A	☐
		Be based on bonus payments	B	☐
		Meet the needs of customers	C	☐
5	Effective customer service transactions are based on the three stages:	Plan, deliver, follow-up	A	☐
		Deliver, follow-up, feedback	B	☐
		Complain, apologise, inform	C	☐

48

2.8 Learning log

Now complete your learning log.

Activity

Learning log for Module 2

Add items to your learning log. When you get to the end of the programme you will need to refine these items to produce a clear action plan.

What I have learned
1
2
3
4
5

Actions planned	Target date
1	
2	
3	
4	
5	

49

Module summary

- Well done – in this module you have learned about different types of customers and how to develop long term, loyal relationships with them. You have identified the key processes that an organisation needs in order to gain the benefits of customer loyalty, and you have learned the importance of planning and following up when dealing with customers.

Module 3: Customer service in different organisations

Module introduction

Welcome to Module 3 of the Best Practice Guide for Customer Service Professionals. In this module we look at several different types of organisations, to see how that changes the approach to delivering high standards of customer service.

3.1 Learning outcomes

When you have successfully read through all the explanations and completed all the activities in this module you will be able to:

- Explain why customer service is important to different types of organisation
- Explain how customer service differs in different types of organisation
- Recognise how the service offer tends to vary for different types of organisations

3.2 The aims of different types organisations

Now we shall look at different types of organisations, starting with their aims. You may work for one of the following types of organisation:

- A profit making organisation
- A not-for-profit organisation
- An organisation with monopoly power

Each type of organisation has different aims. This can affect the customer service that you provide. However every organisation needs excellent customer service. Let us look at the different types of organisations.

Profit making organisations

The main aim of a commercial business is to make profits for its owners or shareholders. The owners or directors of the business plan how to achieve high profits. These plans involve setting objectives for the year ahead. Of course, the owners or directors must communicate their plans to the employees. We shall now look at typical objectives for a profit making organisation. Most of them require excellent customer service.

Now do this activity for organisations within different sectors by completing the next activity.

The service offer ... within different sectors

Here are organisations in three different sectors. Their service offers tend to be very different. Fill in the gaps. Try to think of the services which are offered, rather than the basic product which the customer receives.

Organisation	Typical service offer
A public house	• • • • • •
A bank	• • • • • •
A hairdresser	• • • • •

58

3.4 Moments of truth in different types of organisations

Staying with the theme of different organisations, let us look at what the moments of truth would be for customers of different businesses.

Activity

Moments of truth ... in different organisations	
You are the customer. What, for you, will be a moment of truth for this organisation?	
Organisation	**A moment of truth**
A night club	
A gym or leisure club	
A college	

59

Online retailing or the corner shop?

3.5 Self-assessment

Module 3 Self-assessment

In each case tick the answer that best fits the question.

1	Profit making organisations need	Big bank loans	A	☐
		To establish good reputations for customer service	B	☐
		More competition	C	☐
2	Not-for-profit organisations do not:	Need customer service	A	☐
		Need to balance their books	B	☐
		Always have competitors	C	☐
3	Organisations with monopoly power have:	No competitors	A	☐
		Healthy finances	B	☐
		Satisfied customers	C	☐
4	Added service value is:	Lower costs	A	☐
		Very expensive	B	☐
		Something extra that attracts and keeps customers	C	☐
5	An organisation could improve what it does by:	Benchmarking against other organisations	A	☐
		Increasing sales volumes	B	☐
		Changing its customers	C	☐

3.6 Learning log

Now complete your learning log.

Activity

Learning log for Module 3

Add items to your learning log. When you get to the end of the programme you will need to refine these items to produce a clear action plan.

What I have learned
1
2
3
4
5

Actions planned	Target date
1	
2	
3	
4	
5	

61

Module summary

- Well done – in this module you have learned that organisations can have different aims – they may be profit-makers, not-for-profit organisations or they may have monopoly power. We discussed that all three of these types are under pressure to deliver service excellence. Public sector organisations (like local authorities in the UK or hospitals) may need to improve their reputation through customer service.   A government-appointed regulator can set targets and standards for an organisation that has monopoly power.

  Benchmarking against other organisation is a good way of making sure that service standards in an organisation are as high as possible. We finished the module by looking at how the service offer and moments of truth can be different in the different types of organisations.

Module 4: Match features and benefits

Module introduction

Welcome to Module 4 of the Best Practice Guide for Customer Service Professionals. In this module we explain the difference between the features and the benefits of the products and services that we supply to our customers. We try to match the features and benefits to what the customer wants. You will see how products and service services can be presented to customers so that they know what to expect from your organisation. We also cover the essential selling skills that are used to provide additional products and services to customers

63

4.1   Learning outcomes

When you have successfully read through all the explanations and completed all the activities in this module you will be able to:

- Demonstrate an understanding of features and benefits of products and services that affect the delivery of customer service
- Identify customer preferences and match them to available options
- Recognise how organisations can set product and service standards
- Demonstrate an understanding of equality and diversity issues for an organisation
- Demonstrate an understanding of how to promote additional services or products to customers
- Identify an unique selling point for a product or service

4.2   Your organisation

First things first. To help your external customers, make sure you understand your own organisation. Find out about the basics, if you do not already know them.

Get to know:
- The purpose (or mission) of your organisation
- Its short-term objectives (say for the next year)
- Its long-term objectives (say for the next 5 years)
- Its organisational structure, and where you fit in

4.3 Features and benefits

Think about the organisation's products and services and how these can be matched to customers' needs. Regard all customers as individuals - they like to be treated that way. They each have their own preferences and requirements. As a customer service professional it is your job to ensure you meet these preferences and requirements as best you can.

If you can identify your customers' individual needs, and match your products and services closely to them, then you will satisfy (or delight) your customers and gain a reputation for excellence. It is your reputation that makes a real difference to business success. And that applies to all types of organisation – profit makers, not-for-profit organisations and monopolies.

64

Features of the product/service

Get to know your products and services inside out. Become an expert in what you offer to your customers. You need to understand the features and benefits. Look at these definitions, and then carry out the activity that follows.

Definition Features of a Product or Service	The features of a product or service are its characteristics, such as size, colour, hours of business, power, output, speed and location.

Definition Benefits of a Product or Service	The benefits of a product or service are 'what is in it for the customer', for example it fits into the pocket, co-ordinates with an item of clothing, convenient shopping hours, easy to use, or near public transport.

Meet your customers' preferences

You are a customer service agent dealing with enquiries from customers choosing Personal Computers (PCs). Each PC has a different specification, in other words a different set of features. Some of the product features and some benefits to particular customers have been stated. Where there are gaps, fill them in.

Product/service features		Benefits
Desktop or Laptop	Desktop	Benefit to customer who works in an office or at home
	Laptop	Benefit to customer who travels a lot
Size of hard drive (e.g. 40Gb or 120 Gab)	40Gb	
	120Gb	Benefit to customer who stores large amounts of data – e.g. photos or database
Type & size of monitor (e.g. 15" Flat screen or 17" TFT Panel)	15" Flat screen	Benefit to customer who does mainly word processing
	17" TFT Panel	
Type of CD Drive (e.g. Sony CD-ROM or Sony DVD)	CD-ROM	
	DVD	
Maintenance contract: (e.g. Return to factory or 24-hours a day call-out)	Return to factory	Benefit to customer who does not need immediate repair, such as a home user
	24-hours a day call-out	

65

Try to match your customers' preferences to the specific features and benefits of your product or service. A particular feature may be of benefit to one customer, but of no benefit to another.

Think of the features of package holidays in Spanish hotel resorts. One feature is the location of the hotel. Younger customers tend to choose busy, popular resorts with plenty of clubs and bars. Older customers might prefer a quiet resort without too much noise late at night. (Of course, not all younger and older customers have these preferences). A customer service professional in a travel shop will try to match the type of hotel resort to the preferences of the customer. An older customer who wants a quiet holiday will benefit from a hotel in a quiet resort. If this older customer was sold a holiday in a noisy resort it would be due to a failure to match his or her individual preferences to the features and benefits of the package holiday.

66

Matching the product or service to the preferences of the customer

Features and Benefits

Choose a product or service that is offered to customers of your organisation (or one that you are familiar with). The product may have add-on services included. (For example, an electrical product like a refrigerator includes add-on services such as: finance, next-day delivery, and repair under guarantee). List some features and benefits of your product or service (or one that you are familiar with) below.

Product or Service:

Features	Benefits

Make the best of features and benefits

Now think carefully about how you use features and benefits. Give an example of how you make the best of your features and benefits to help your customers.

Of course you can use features and benefits wrongly. Give an example of how you might damage the service given to your customers by using features and benefits in the wrong way.

67

4.4 Product and service standards

Match your products and services to your customers' needs by keeping to standards. Standards should ideally be written down so that customers know what to expect. (Make sure that you understand the difference between product standards and service standards).

Product standards describe key features of the product. These often appear in catalogues and brochures that are used to promote the product. Once the customer has bought the product the product standards are often provided in more detail. For example, if you buy a personal computer you will receive with it the product specification - details of the hardware and software components, which versions, what performance you can expect, and so on. These are product standards.

Service standards are just as important. The customer needs to know what service to expect along with the product itself. The best business organisations have clear service standards. These are written statements. They show the level of service that customers can expect, and the level of service that employees need to provide. For example if you order goods from a website you should be told how long the goods will take to arrive. This is a service standard.

Service standards have these advantages:
- Organisational and personal standards help us to provide excellent customer service
- Standards are a guide to help you do your job
- Standards help to ensure consistent levels of service
- Standards help you to measure the effectiveness of your customer service

Some sectors and organisations publish a customer charter. This is also a way of letting the customers know what to expect.

Definition	A customer charter is a statement of intent and is generally not part of the contract that a service deliverer makes with its customer.
Customer charter	

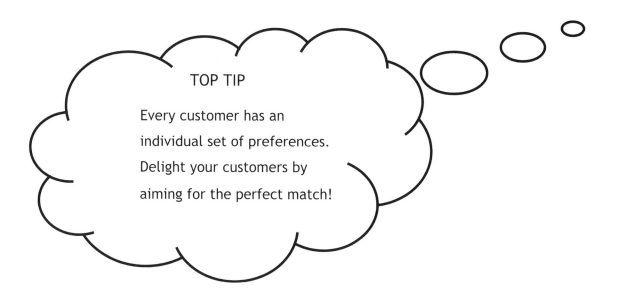

TOP TIP

Every customer has an individual set of preferences. Delight your customers by aiming for the perfect match!

69

In the next activity, think about your own service standards, and those of your organisation.

What are your service standards?

List three service standards that apply to your own customer service

1	
2	
3	

Does your organisation have any statements or charters setting out the standards of service that customers can expect? If so, what aspects do they cover?

Try creating some service standards yourself by completing the next activity.

Create service standards

For this activity put yourself in the role of a customer service agent working for a large, national furniture retailer. The retailer has branches in many cities and towns across the UK. The company wants to set service standards, because some customers have complained recently.

Following a television advertising campaign, sales of certain sofas and beds increased dramatically. However, the furniture manufacturers could not meet the delivery deadlines, and so some customers did not receive their furniture orders within the delivery guideline of six weeks. Some customers who ordered Italian leather sofas had to wait over four months for their furniture to arrive. This is damaging the reputation of the company. Not only that - when complaints were made they were not handled well, and some customers then cancelled their orders.

You have been asked by your supervisor to give your views on what service standards could be put into place. Write down three service standards which would be relevant to customers of this business. For each one, describe what actions would need to be taken to make sure the company can meet these service standards.

	Service standard	Actions needed to meet standards
1		
2		
3		

4.5 Welcome diverse customers and colleagues

Equality and diversity is about the day-to-day issues that affect people: our differences, our similarities, how we communicate and how we relate to each other.

The law requires organisations to create a `level playing field' in the workplace. Individuals, irrespective of their race, sex or disability should have equal access to employment opportunities and the services that different organisations provide.  The law plays an important part in ensuring that `the rules of the game' are fair.

Legislation

There is a range of legislation that affects equality and diversity, including:

- The Sex Discrimination Act 1975 and the 2003 Sex Discrimination (Gender Re-assignment) regulations
- The Disability Discrimination Act 1995
- The Race Relations Act 1976 and the Race Relations (Amendment) Act 2000
- The Special Educational Needs and Disabilities Act (SENDA) 2001
- The Equal Pay Act 1970/84
- Race and Employment Directives of 2000 agreed with the European Union in 1997 [The Treaty of Amsterdam] to implement Article 13 of the Human Rights Act (2000/43/EC).
- The Equal Treatment Directive of 1976 for men and women (1976/207/EEC) and of 2000 for religion or belief, disability, age or sexual orientation (2000/78/EC).

Refer to Module 8: Laws and codes of practice, for further information about laws affecting sex discrimination and race relations.

The purpose of this legislation is to ensure that people are treated fairly and equally at work, in terms of recruitment and employment conditions. An employer must take account of all the legislation. Organisations must have policies, procedures and working practices that ensure fairness, respect and equal treatment for everyone. As a customer service professional you should know and understand the implications of this legislation.

How it can go wrong

Discrimination and harassment could occur under the headings below.

Age You should not treat someone unfairly or harass them because they are seen as being too old or too young.

Ethnicity, religion and culture Treating someone unfairly or harassing them because of where they, or their family, originate from, or because of their faith, culture or skin colour; or failing to respect their religious or philosophical beliefs would be seen as discrimination.

Sexual orientation and Trans-sexuality People should not be treated unfairly or harassed because they are a gay man, a lesbian, bisexual or transgender.

Gender Ensure that people are not treated unfairly or harassed because they are male or female.

Disability There is a wide range of disabilities. Treating people unfairly or harassing them if they have a disability such as a sensory or mobility impairment, a form of disfigurement, or a learning or mental health problem must not happen.

Diversity

Diversity relates to every aspect of human culture, outlook and experience. To some extent, we all have our own opinions on some or all of the core aspects of diversity - be it gender, race, religion, sexual orientation, age or disability. But the important thing to remember is not all of them are going to be right or appropriate in today's highly diverse society and that sometimes it is necessary to separate our attitudes from our public behaviour. Treat the people you deal with professionally, as customers. If you do that, you will recognise their needs and differences as individuals.

The difference between equality and diversity

You have heard and read about "equality and diversity." The two concepts go together but are different. Diversity initiatives go further than equal opportunities. They aim to take people's diverse characteristics fully into account and to get maximum benefit from their uniqueness as individuals.

Diversity recognises that each of us is different and unique. That uniqueness is made up of a mix of visible and non-visible individual characteristics. Consequently, it makes sense that treating everyone the same is not necessarily going to work. Different people will have different aspirations, expectations, opportunities, responsibilities and needs. Therefore treating people fairly means recognising those differences, respecting them and acting accordingly. An organisation that values diversity not only has a strong sense of social justice but also sees the business benefits of pursuing good equality and diversity strategies. In short, diversity is about valuing differences.

Organisations cannot afford to ignore large sections of the population. People from diverse backgrounds, age groups, etc. may be attracted to a particular organisation because of its reputation for equality and its respect for people. This includes customers as well as employees.

Ensure that people are not treated unfairly or harassed because they are male or female

In your customer service role, try to recognise all forms of diversity amongst your customers. Respond to their individual needs and expectations. Look for signs of diversity. These signs could include dress, appearance, accent, behaviour and many others. Get used to recognising both verbal and non-verbal clues that show the individuality of your customers. Use these clues to become really responsive to your customers. However, be careful not to stereotype your customers. Not all people from one country or culture adopt the religion or customs of that country. Not all people who have a hearing impediment need to be treated in the same way. Be vary careful not to make assumptions about people – they might be offended if the assumptions are wrong! Use your questioning skills and your active listening skills to find out more about the individual need of customers. But again, be careful to make sure your questions are tactful and respectful. Keep everything on a professional level. Your aim is to help customers identify the products and service which they can benefit from, and to make the transaction easy to carry out from their point of view.

Find out about your organisation's approach to equality and diversity. Read the equal opportunities policy and get advice on how to deal with customers by following your organisation's guidelines. Discuss with colleagues how you can adopt a really inclusive approach to gain maximum benefit from meeting all your customers' expectations.

74

Equality and Diversity Checklist

Do you adopt best practice in Equality and Diversity? Answer the following questions honestly and see if you can improve your responsiveness to diversity.

Are you familiar with your organisation's policies and procedures for Equality and Diversity?		
Do you treat your internal and external customers fairly and with respect?		
List the groups of customers to whom you regularly provide customer service.		
What behaviours should you avoid so as not to offend to these groups of customers?		
Can a wide range of customers with disabilities or impairments access your products and services?		
Think of three actions you can take to be more inclusive and responsive to the needs of these groups of customers.	1	
	2	
	3	

75

4.6 Sell or promote products and services to your customers

Every organisation communicates, persuades and negotiates with customers. These are the skills needed for selling products and services. To enhance your skills as a customer service professional, learn how to sell to your customers. Even if your main role is not selling, you will find many opportunities to introduce additional products and services to your customers. These can enhance your customers' satisfaction.

The benefits of selling additional products and services

In your role as a customer service professional you match your products and services to your customers' needs. In a profit making organisation this means selling to your customers to enhance profits. Even in not-for-profit and public sector organisations it can be of benefit to sell or promote additional products and services.

The benefits of selling or promoting of additional products include:

- For a profit-maker, higher profits through increased sales
- For a public sector or not-for-profit organisation, healthier finances through increased revenue
- For customers, increased satisfaction
- For any organisation, enhanced reputation and customer loyalty through higher customer satisfaction

Know your organisation's procedures

First of all, make sure you know your organisation's procedures for selling or promoting additional products and services. Whether or not you are a sales person you should learn how your organisation wants you to deal with this aspect of your customer service role. To help you do this, complete the next activity.

Activity

Procedures for selling or promoting

Find out how your organisation wants you sell promote additional products and services to your customers. You can include customers asking for further information. For the procedures that apply to you, just make a note of the procedure, if there is one. Then briefly say what you should do.

Offering additional products	
Offering additional service	
Giving further information	
Referring onto someone else	

Know your products and services

The first priority is to know your products and services. Learn them inside out. If your organisation has hundreds of products you cannot expect to know them all – but try to become an expert advisor for your customers. Learn how and where to find the answers to your customers' questions. Discover who to refer them to if you cannot answer their questions. (Remember, though, that customers prefer to deal with as few people as possible. They will soon become frustrated if they are passed from pillar to post).

Remember that nobody buys just the product or service. They buy the benefits that ownership brings. Benefits are often emotional as well as logical and it is those benefits that encourage customers to part with their money.

The phrase to remember for selling is "people buy people." Customers are interested in your additional products and services if they are interested in you. If they relate to you they will listen to what you have to say.

Know your products and services

Here are your guide-lines for successful selling:

Guide-lines for successful selling

- Create a good first impression – with a selling environment that is well presented and clean
- Be knowledgeable and passionate about your products and services
- "People buy people" - so feel positive about yourself
- Get the first few seconds right - observe your customers' body language to choose the best time to approach them
- Show an interest in your customers and show them you care
- Build a rapport with the customer by choosing the best way to start the conversation
- Observe everything that is happening around you, particularly customers who might be in a hurry
- Make it personal by remembering names, likes and dislikes if you can
- Ask the right questions and listen carefully to the customer's answers so that you can identify their requirements
- Demonstrate the features and benefits of your products and services,
- Emphasise the Unique Selling Points (USPs)
- Close the sale and follow through – do not promise what you cannot deliver
- Challenge yourself every day, set yourself a target to learn something new about your customers or your product range

4.7 Self-assessment

Module 4 Self-assessment				
In each case tick the answer that best fits the question.				
1	The benefits of a product or service are:	What's in it for the organisation	A	☐
		What's in it for the customer	B	☐
		What's in it for you	C	☐
2	A specific feature of a product or service is likely to be:	A benefit for nobody	A	☐
		A benefit for all customers	B	☐
		More of a benefit for some customers than others	C	☐
3	Some organisations publish a customer charter. This is so that:	Customers know how to complain	A	☐
		Customers know what to expect of the organisation	B	☐
		Customers know the prices of the organisation's products	C	☐
4	The law requires organisations to:	Create a level playing field in the workplace	A	☐
		Pay all employees the same wages or salaries	B	☐
		Treat all employees in the same way	C	☐
5	Diversity is a concept which recognises that:	Everyone is the same	A	☐
		Everyone has different needs and aspirations	B	☐
		Everyone is on a different rate of pay	C	☐

4.8   Learning log

Now complete your learning log.

Learning log for Module 4

Add items to your learning log. When you get to the end of the programme you will need to refine these items to produce a clear action plan.

What I have learned
1
2
3
4
5

Actions planned	Target date
1	
2	
3	
4	
5	

84

Module summary

- Well done – in this module you have learned the difference between features and benefits. Features are part of the product or service, and benefits are "what is in it for the customer." You have understood the importance of trying to match the features and benefits to what the customer wants – in order to produce satisfied, loyal customers.

We then looked at product and service standards as a way of helping the customer to make the best choice for him or her. A customer charter is one example of how these standards can be made available to customers. In the final activity of the module you created your own service standards and planned actions to meet those standards.

You considered how you and your organisation deal with the important issues relating to equality and diversity. You have learned the importance of selling skills for all customer service professionals. You know how to use your listening and observation skills. When you introduce products and services you know how to explain their benefits and close the sale.

85

Module 5: Communicate effectively

Module introduction

Welcome to Module 5 of the Best Practice Guide for Customer Service Professionals. In this module we look at all aspects of communication. You will learn the importance of effective communication when you deal with internal customers as well as external customers. We cover guidelines for improving your communication skills.

5.1 Learning outcomes

When you have successfully read through all the explanations and completed all the activities in this module you will be able to:

- Describe the importance of effective communication in the delivery of customer service
- Choose the most appropriate communication method to suit a specific customer service situation
- Recognise the value of effective verbal and non-verbal communication skills in customer service transactions
- Choose behaviour that is appropriate to a specific customer service situation
- Understand the benefits, features and methods of using information and communications technology (ICT) in order to deliver effective customer service

5.2 Why it is important to communicate well

You and your organisation must communicate effectively in order to provide service excellence. Remember that communication is a two-way process. The two way communication process needs to work well in a number of different areas.

Internal communication

Internal communication must work well inside the organisation. Your organisation should have effective communication in these areas:

- From managers to staff and from staff to managers
- Between people in different departments

- Between people in different branches (if there are branches in more than one location)
- Between people within the same department

Communicating effectively

External communication

Make sure that you, your colleagues and managers communicate well with people outside the organisation, such as:

- Existing customers
- Potential new customers
- Past customers (who may become customers again)
- Suppliers
- Stakeholders (for example community groups, local authorities, local councils or shareholders)

Communication often goes wrong. It is the root of many problems. It can also be the best way to solve problems once they have occurred. If you communicate well with your customers then you have the basis of an excellent, long term customer relationship.
It is a common mistake to concentrate too much on the "talking" aspect of communication. But you cannot communicate unless you listen effectively as well.

Internal communication must work well inside the organisation

5.3 Choose and use the appropriate communication methods

Choose the best method of communication, not just for you, but for the customer. There is not always a choice. If a customer telephones you, then you have to communicate effectively on the telephone. However, sometimes you do have a choice of communication method. Do you email a customer, or telephone them? If you are promoting your product or service, should you do this in a newspaper advertisement, by sending out flyers or by using a website? Put yourself in the position of the customer. Make your decision according to what would work best for the customer.

Get to recognise the pros and cons of each method of communication. That way, you will choose the right method. Just as important, you will recognise how best to use that method.

Adapt your method and style of communication to the situation you are in. Again, think of the customer. If the customer is coming in to make a complaint, do not have a broad grin on your face. If a customer wants reassurance about your promise to contact them once you have sorted out a problem, use appropriate body language to help you get the point across. (We will study body language as part of non-verbal communication in section 5.5).

Let us look at some common communication methods, and how they are best used by a customer service professional.

5.4 Face to face communication

Face to face communication is the most effective and reliable form of communication. You can see and hear each other, and use the full range of language and signals to get your point across. You can use your listening skills to gain valuable information from your customers.

Use the face to face method whenever you can. If there is a serious complaint or problem to deal with, try to get to see the customer to sort it out. It is better to do that than to try solving the problem by telephone or email. Of course, time, cost and distance often mean that a face to face meeting is impossible.

89

When you do meet face to face adopt a positive and professional approach at all times.

Be emotionally sensitive to the customer

Use the following guide lines for speaking face to face with your customers:

Face-to-face guide-lines

- Dress professionally, in line with your organisation's dress code
- Be positive and friendly, and smile
- Be aware of your standing or sitting posture, so that you do not appear threatening, disinterested or frustrated
- Greet your customer in a welcoming way
- Speak clearly without being monotonous
- If you are discussing a problem, stay professional - calm and positive
- Be emotionally sensitive to the customer - use your skills of empathy - put yourself in the customer's shoes to appreciate the situation from their point of view
- If the customer does become angry or difficult, stay calm and resist the temptation to argue, shout or be defensive

5.5 Effective non-verbal communication

It is thought that around 60% of face-to-face communication is done without speaking. Your appearance, posture, face, eyes, hands, arms, legs and gestures all give clear messages to the customer. Not everybody recognises that body language is happening, but everybody uses it. Many people communicate using body language without even realising it.

Definition	Body language is a collection of expressions on our face and gestures we make using our hands and body.
Body Language	

Use non-verbal communication effectively and positively to help the customer and add to your professionalism. Do not allow your body language to send mixed messages, or to give the wrong impression to your customer.

To help you here are some body language dos and don'ts:

Body language Dos and Don'ts		
	Do	Don't
Body posture	• Sit up • Face the customer	• Lean back • Fold your arms • Slouch
Eye contact	• Maintain eye contact with the customer	• Glare at the customer • Roll your eyes upwards • Look away at difficult moments
Facial expression	• Present a bright appearance • Smile often (when appropriate) • Show concern (when appropriate)	• Look bored, fed up or angry
Gestures & mannerisms	• Be aware of what you are doing with your hands • Be aware of your own mannerisms	• Fidget or do anything to look bored • Keep checking your watch • Point at the customer

91

TO GET YOU THINKING

Discuss with a colleague how you use non-verbal communication with your own customers. During the discussion, watch how your partner uses body language. After the discussion give your partner feedback

5.6 Body image

To help you create a good impression with your customers you need to present the right image. Look the part of the professional. Your dress and general appearance are important for your customers. At a moment of truth the way you look can make the difference in keeping the customer loyal. It's not just superficial – the customer will form an impression from limited information, especially if the customer only has a fleeting contact with you.

Don't point at the customer

To look the part of the customer service professional, follow these guidelines:

Body image guide-lines

- Dress smartly and professionally
- Follow your employer's dress code
- Keep your clothes looking good
- Wash or shower regularly – and more frequently if you play sport or use a gym
- Keep your hair in good condition
- If you wear jewellery ensure it fits with your company's dress code
- If you have tattoos you may need to keep them covered up – your customers will be of all ages and attitudes and some may not be impressed! The same applies for unusual body piercings

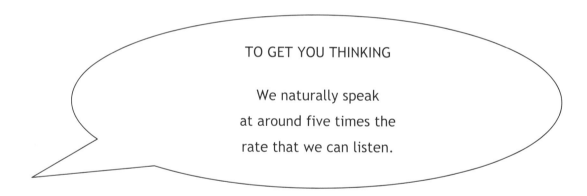

TO GET YOU THINKING

We naturally speak
at around five times the
rate that we can listen.

5.7 Active listening skills

To raise your game as a customer service professional you need to use active listening skills. We naturally speak faster than we can listen. To listen effectively you must make a conscious, planned effort to apply some very specific listening skills.

When you are in conversation with your customer it is easy to talk, but even more important to listen. You must ask the right questions and use the right techniques to ensure that you really do understand your customer's needs and expectations.

Listen with an open mind, particularly when there has been a misunderstanding. You need to reassure the customer that you have fully understood their point of view. Remember that listening can be hard work and requires concentration. It is a skill that can be developed but it will gain you valuable customer feedback which you can use to improve the service that you provide.

Effective non-verbal communication

Use the following simple guide-lines when talking and listening to your customers. Remember that this applies just as much to your internal customers, as well as your external customers.

Guide-lines for Active Listening Skills

- Hold your customer conversations in a convenient, comfortable environment
- When talking and listening to a customer, try to remove all distractions
- Be clear what information you want from your customer
- Plan your questions or use a prepared script
- Start your conversation by chatting or relaxing your customer – remember that customers may be nervous of someone in authority
- Note down answers if appropriate using paper or computer
- Be positive in your questioning
- Encourage clear answers by using the right body language
- Confirm you understand by using phrases like "I see", "oh yes" and "that's clear now"
- If you do not understand, use phrases like "Can you explain that further" and "What did you mean exactly by ..."
- Listen for what the customer really wants and feels – this is often different from what he/she actually says
- Re-affirm the information you have gathered at stages during the conversation and at the end
- Make sure you record and/or pass on the information you have gathered
- Thank your customer at the end of the conversation
- Agree what will happen next

95

Now work out where you need to improve your listening skills in the following activity.

Activity

Improve your listening skills

This activity will help you identify your strengths and areas for improvement when listening. For each statement tick the box that most accurately reflects your skill level.

	Listening skill	I do this very well	I do this fairly well	I could improve this	I need to improve this a lot
1	When I am listening I try to remove all distractions	☐	☐	☐	☐
2	I think carefully about the information I want to find out when asking questions	☐	☐	☐	☐
3	I listen carefully to everything a person wants to say before drawing my own conclusions	☐	☐	☐	☐
4	I recognise and acknowledge my own and other peoples' emotions	☐	☐	☐	☐
5	I am pleased to deal with people who have values that are different from my own	☐	☐	☐	☐
6	When people appear angry or aggressive, I listen carefully to understand the real message underneath	☐	☐	☐	☐
7	When I am listening and feel upset or anxious myself, I try hard to control my own emotions	☐	☐	☐	☐
8	When dealing with difficult situations or difficult people, I try hard to resolve the situation positively	☐	☐	☐	☐
9	I listen well to people whose accents or ethnic backgrounds differ from mine	☐	☐	☐	☐
10	I let other people finish what they want to say before making my own points	☐	☐	☐	☐
11	I use body language to show other people that I am listening and interested in what they have to say	☐	☐	☐	☐
12	I summarise what has been said and agreed so that the person knows that I have understood	☐	☐	☐	☐

Make a plan for how you are going to improve your listening skills by completing the next activity.

Listening skills improvement plan

Add up the number of ticks in each of the four columns. How many did you score?

	Score		Score
I do this very well		I do this reasonably well	
I could improve this		I need to improve this a lot	

Write down the actions you will take to make the improvements that are needed.

| |
| |

97

5.8 Use behaviour appropriate to the situation

Try to use the right behaviour with your customers. To do this you will need to recognise the emotional state and needs of your customers. A customer service professional is in tune with the emotions of his or her customers. You should also be aware of your own emotions and how they can affect your relationships with customers. (Later on in the Best Practice Guide, in Module 9, you will study Emotional intelligence – this will give more detailed information on how to deal with your customers' and your own emotions).

Most of your customer transactions will be straightforward. However, in some cases your customer may be disappointed, upset, frustrated, angry, depressed or even vindictive. As a professional you must react in the best possible way to the customer. This means that you have to "get inside the customer's head", to try to see it from their point of view. If you can do that you will be far more capable of sorting out the problem.

Try to get your attitude right. Behave in a way that is appropriate to the situation.

- If the customer is new to your business and is making an enquiry about your products and services, be bright positive and keen to explain the benefits
- If the customer needs you to progress the transaction to the next stage, be very business-like and explain, step by step what will happen
- If the customer has a problem, listen attentively, be sympathetic and recognise that the problem is there. Then try to help solve it
- If the customer is angry, keep calm and try to stay positive and as friendly as possible to reduce the need for his or her anger
- If the customer is very angry, or even abusive, you may need to be decisive and call a halt to the conversation before it gets worse
- There are no golden rules – except "stay professional at all times"

You may find that a basic form of Transactional Analysis is useful when you are dealing with customers. Here is a definition:

Transactional Analysis

Transactional analysis was developed by Dr Eric Berne in the 1950s. It can help you when you are dealing with customers. Think of two people communicating. The person who sends the first message is sending the transactional stimulus. The person who replies is carrying out a transactional response.

Definition Transactional Analysis	Transactional Analysis is a framework for describing behaviour in an interchange between two people. It helps you to understand why customers react the way they do especially when you are dealing with a problem.

Transactional analysis looks at the ego states of the two people communicating. We can identify three ego states: Adult, Child and Parent. The meanings of these ego states are as follows:

Adult

The Adult ego state is about being spontaneous and aware. When in our Adult we are able to see people as they are, rather than what we project onto them.

98

Child

The Child ego state is a set of behaviours, thoughts and feelings which are replayed from our own childhood. Perhaps the boss calls us into his or her office, we may immediately get a churning in our stomach and wonder what we have done wrong.

Parent

This is behaviour that we have copied from our parents. As we grow up we take in ideas, beliefs, feelings and behaviours from our parents and carers. For example, we may notice that we are saying things just as our father or mother may have done.

If one of the two people is a customer complaining, that customer will have one of the three ego states Adult, Child or Parent.

Be aware in your customer conversations of the transactional stimulus. If this comes from the customer decide whether it is Adult, Child or Parent. If the stimulus is Parent try not to give a Child response. Your aim should be to turn all communications into Adult – Adult ones.

99

Activity

Ego states	
A customer is complaining to a customer service agent. In each of the situations below say what ego state you think the complainer is in.	
Customer complaint	**Ego state of customer**
It's a disgrace!	
It's not fair.	
Can you tell me why this delivery is taking so long?	

A simple example of Transactional Analysis

Study the following example.

" *Your terms of service say the sofa will be delivered in 3 weeks. It is now 4 weeks. Can you explain why?*"   (Adult)

" *Yes delivery should be 21 days. I am sorry for the delay and I will make sure that the order is being processed.*"   (Adult)

However, if you reply as follows:

"You will have to speak to the despatch department. I don't deal with after sales."

...you will probably get a Child response hitting back at a Parent - which causes a crossed transaction.

Crossed transactions can occur by reading comments into messages that are not there. This can lead to really heated exchanges! However it is possible to uncross a transaction. Look at this example.

"This shirt you sold me is a disgrace and is falling to pieces."   (Parent)

... this is a Parent to Child comment.

If the reply comes from an Adult then the crossed transaction can be stopped in its tracks, as follows:

"I'm sorry sir. Let me change it for you."   (Adult)

Try having a conversation with someone where you alter your ego state to Parent or Child and notice the outcome. Similarly try changing a conversation to an Adult ego state where it has been started as a Parent or Child one.

5.9 Communicating on the telephone

Talking effectively with your customers on the telephone is essential. You have to make that first impression count. Then you must follow through to make sure the customer's needs are met. If possible, try to go further, and exceed your customer's expectations.

Dealing with some customers on the telephone can be difficult. They may be unhappy. You have to provide a sympathetic ear, and efficiently solve the problem. Of course, you may have to call them back or refer the issue to your supervisor, but this too must be done in the right way.

You might deal with customers who find it hard to understand your speech or accent. Speak very clearly and more slowly if this happens. Remain patient. Adapt your speed of speech, your tone and the words you use to your customers. Ask your colleagues to help if they can. Remember that it is your job to respond to your individual customers, and this includes varying what you say and how you say it.

Use the following 8-stage technique as a framework for dealing with customers on the telephone.

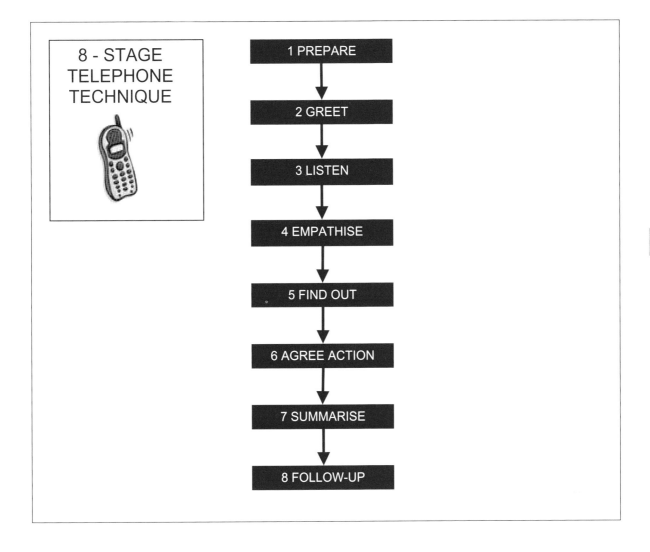

101

Stage 1 : Prepare

Prepare well for your telephone calls. Remember how annoying it can be when you are talking to someone on the telephone and they say "Hang on a minute, I'll just try to find a pen", or "Just a second, I'll go and get the file".

Preparing to take or make calls involves:
- Have you notepad/pencil/computer screen ready
- Have any information you know that you will need to hand
- Concentrate on what you need to do during the call, removing any distractions
- Make sure you have all the resources you need before you make the call - for example, if you know you are likely to have to refer to your supervisor, ensure he or she will be there at the time of the call
- Make sure you are comfortable with the handset, desk, computer screen, ear phones and your own posture
- Ensure you know how to use the mute feature of the handset, so that, if you need to, you can talk to your nearby colleagues in privacy while the customer is still on the line

Stage 2 : Greet

Find out about your organisation's procedures and guidelines for talking to customers on the telephone. You should be trained or coached on these procedures if they exist.

You may have been trained to use a standard greeting, for example, "ABC Sales Desk. This is Sonja speaking. How may I help you?" If you use a standard greeting, follow this advice:
- The worst thing you can do is say the standard greeting as if you are bored with it. You may have repeated it thousands of times already, but to that customer it conveys important information. Be friendly, lively but business-like, and use a positive tone of voice, which convinces the customer that you are there to provide help.
- Don't rush through the greeting too quickly - you are familiar with it but your customer is not.
- To ensure that your voice comes across as positive and friendly, try smiling! Believe it or not if you smile on the telephone the customer at the end of the line can tell.

If there is no standard greeting, you need to use one which will be effective, telling the customer who is on the line, what your role/organisation is and giving confidence that you are there to help.

Stage 3 : Listen

Listen carefully to what the caller is saying, and if you discover you cannot deal with the issue yourself politely interrupt and pass the call to the appropriate person. If you do this ensure that you pass on the information that the customer has given you. We all dislike having to repeat the same information.

Ask questions clearly to find out all you need to complete the transaction.

Stage 4 : Empathise

Empathise with the customer, be sincere and positive in trying to find out what is wanted. If the customer has a problem, do not take it personally.

Be responsive and caring if there are problems – start your response with phrases like "I can understand the problem you have…" or "Yes I can see that this hasn't been done as it should…"

Do not use phrases like "I don't see how I can help…" or "What do you want me to do…"

You may occasionally have to talk to an angry or abusive customer. Find out (before this happens) what you organisation's procedure is for this. If you have to refer it to a colleague you need to know who that is. If you have a standard procedure once the customer becomes abusive, learn it and practice it so that you can use it comfortably when you need to.

103

Stage 5 : Find out

Your questioning skills will develop with time and practice, but be aware that you should try to control the call through a combination of effective questioning and efficient choice of what should happen next.

You need to ask the right questions in order to:
- establish the facts
- find out what needs to be done
- enable you to deal with the matter effectively and speedily
- reassure the customer that you are dealing with the matter

Ask clear questions, either:
- Closed questions (requiring a yes or no answer), or
- Open questions (with which you allow the customer to explain or expand)

Stage 6 : Agree action

Once you have the information you need, be decisive and agree with the customer what will happen next.

Don't be tempted to put the matter off, just to move onto your next call – you must deal with this customer and complete as much of the transaction as possible immediately. On the other hand, don't promise now what you cannot deliver – this will cause problems later.

Don't pass the customer onto anyone else unless you really have to – nobody likes being passed on, because it wastes time and reduces the customer's confidence in you and your organisation.

Make certain (by further questions) that the customer does agree with what you propose.

Explain your agreed action in clear stages, so that the customer knows exactly what to expect.

Stage 7 : Summarise

Summarise simply to the customer what the situation is and what is going to happen next. If possible, include timescales.

Stage 8 : Follow-up

The follow-up work (if there is any) is absolutely vital. Make good notes so that you will now not forget what you have agreed to do. If the follow-up involves colleagues ensure that you explain clearly, with notes, what should happen. Remember that the follow-up is a kind of contract between you and the customer – don't let them down. The follow-up is your opportunity as a customer service professional, to complete the job to a high standard and thereby keep the customer loyal.

Try the following activity to improve your telephone greeting technique.

Telephone greetings

Review the following telephone greetings and write down any good and bad points.

	Greeting	Your comments
1	"Customer service, this is Fiona."	
2	"Good morning, Roger speaking."	
3	"Good morning, James Brothers Transport, Dispatch Desk. This is Damien, how may I help you?"	
4	"Just hang on please, I'll be with you shortly."	
5	"Hi there, Jason here, what can I do you for?"	
6	"Hello, this is the Sales Department, whom did you want to speak to?"	
7	"Hi, how can I help?"	

5.10 Email, letter and fax

Email is a common method of communication. Letters are still required however, because many customers do not have access to email. Also, letters are regarded by some people as more "official." If you have to confirm something with a customer, then generally you will need to do it "in writing." But remember to keep it personal if possible, particularly if you are responding to a complaint. There is nothing worse than a standard letter to make your complainant really angry. The fax is also a convenient method of sending and receiving

5.13 Self-assessment

Module 5 Self-assessment

In each case tick the answer that best fits the question.

1	Face to face communication is the most:	Used form of communication	A	☐
		Reliable form of communication	B	☐
		Unreliable form of communication	C	☐
2	Being emotionally sensitive to your customer means that you:	Reflect the mood of the customer	A	☐
		Appreciate the situation from the customer's point of view	B	☐
		Are likely to get upset when dealing with customers	C	☐
3	Body language is:	Expressions on our face and gestures we make using our hands and body	A	☐
		Using hand movements to get the point across	B	☐
		Used mainly for hearing impaired customers	C	☐
4	Communication by email has the advantage of being:	A good way of expressing your feelings	A	☐
		A good way of getting an immediate answer	B	☐
		A good way of providing the same information to a group of people	C	☐
5	Websites can be effective for giving customers:	The wrong impression of your company	A	☐
		Helpful and easily accessible information	B	☐
		The personal touch	C	☐

112

5.14 Learning log

Now complete your learning log.

Activity

Learning log for Module 5

Add items to your learning log. When you get to the end of the programme you will need to refine these items to produce a clear action plan.

What I have learned
1
2
3
4
5

Actions planned	Target date
1	
2	
3	
4	
5	

Module summary

- Well done – in this module you have identified the importance of effective communication in order to meet and exceed customers' expectations. You have seen a framework which may be used for dealing with customers on the telephone, and you may have planned out some specific actions to put into place in order to improve your listening skills. As well as the traditional communication methods you have learned about body language and electronic forms such as websites and emails.

Module 6: Deliver service excellence through teamwork

Module introduction

Welcome to Module 6 of the Best Practice Guide for Customer Service Professionals. In this module we discuss why effective teams are best for you and your customers. You will clearly recognise the benefits of team working and understand how to contribute to the teams that you belong to. You also had the chance to use a checklist to test how well your team is doing.

6.1 Learning outcomes

115

When you have successfully read through all the explanations and completed all the activities in this module you will be able to:

- Demonstrate an understanding of effective methods of team working in the delivery of customer service
- Identify examples of working in partnership with other organisations

6.2 The need for teamwork

At work everyone performs as part of a team. Many people belong to more than one team. In your customer service role you can identify the team that you are a member of. Try the first activity in this module.

Case Study: Every second counts!

Think of a Formula One motor racing team. It is the ideal situation for team working. For weeks and months before the race the team works hard on the car. They are getting it ready for the day, and setting it up with great precision for the driver. During the practice sessions and during the race itself the team members all have their own roles to play.

When the driver comes in for a pit stop every second counts! Each team member performs their own task as quickly as possible. It must be done with perfect timing, to work in harmony with the rest of the team. How does the Formula One team do this so effectively? Through training, understanding what the customer (the driver in this case) wants, and through practice.

Apply the principles of the Formula One pit team to your own job. Work with your colleagues to understand exactly how to deliver service excellence. Practice your processes and procedures so that, when the customer turns up, your team can perform to perfection. Perfect your team working to win!

6.3 The benefits of teamwork

You should enjoy working as part of your team. If you enjoy it you will do it better. Naturally, sometimes teams have difficulties. Members of the team may become de-motivated and not work effectively for the team. If things go wrong people may start blaming other team members for the problems. It is better to share most problems with the team, and gain the support of colleagues to try to solve the problems. In fact, this is one of the key benefits of team working - using others to help you with problems and difficulties.

Teams of customer service professionals need to be clear about the team's overall objectives. There should be a shared vision of service excellence. All the members know that the prime objective is to deliver excellent service to the customers, and how this is to be done.

As we have said, many people work in several teams. You may work in a team of customer service agents for example. But also you pass information onto other departments, for instance so that the customer's payment can be handled by the finance department. If the customer complains at some stage this may be handled by yet another team. Therefore another benefit of team working is that people in different departments and parts of the business can deliver more effective service.

People at work like to be involved. Some people may be better team players than others, but nevertheless we all benefit from being involved with other people. A sense of involvement tends to motivate people. Everyone in the organisation can ultimately be involved in delivering service excellence to the customer.

To summarise the main benefits of team working:

- The team has shared objectives
- Better knowledge of others' job roles
- Enjoyment of working with others
- Increased involvement, job satisfaction and motivation
- Someone to help out when there are deadlines to meet
- Better communication between departments

6.4 Satisfy your internal customers

Treat your internal customers the way you should treat your external customers. They are just as important. If you communicate with and work with your internal customers well, you will be working more effectively as a team.

Just as an external customer will feel delighted if you go the extra mile for them, so will your internal customers. You yourself will establish your own personal reputation as someone who really cares and does a professional job within the organisation.

6.5 Working in partnership with other organisations

Remember that external customers are not just the ones who come to you for your products and services. Suppliers and other partner organisations that you deal with are also external customers. Your organisation probably works in partnership with many organisations. Try the next activity. It may help you to deliver service excellence to the partners that you work with outside of your organisation.

Activity

See your partners as your customers

List up to five partners (organisations or individual people) that you deal with in your customer service role. For each partner, say briefly what you will have to do to delight them as external customers.

	Partner	How to provide service excellence
1		
2		
3		
4		
5		

TOP TIP

Turn your external partners into ambassadors for your organisation – by giving them excellent customer service.

6.6 Clear principles of team working

When you work as part of a team, make sure that you keep to the following principles. For an effective team, you need:

- SMART team objectives (SMART is usually taken to mean: Specific, Measurable, Achievable, Realistic and Time-constrained)
- well defined roles for every team member
- agreed standards and procedures
- good communication between the team members

It is not just the responsibility of the team leader or manager to ensure that these principles are present. It is depends upon you and your colleagues.

121

Quote from ...	"Give support to each other and praise more than criticise." (Johnston, 2003)
Tesco	

Now here are your team working Dos and Don'ts:

Team working Dos and Don'ts	
Do	**Don't**
<ul><li>Take time in your team to review and improve how the team operates</li><li>Make sure the team's objectives are clear</li><li>Make sure your own objectives are clear</li><li>Talk regularly about who will do what and by when</li><li>Work together as much as possible when you are trying solve customers' problems</li><li>Make sure that your team members all communicate well</li><li>Have short, sharp team meetings to give everyone a chance to air their views and suggest improvements</li><li>Stay involved and try to keep all the other team members involved</li><li>Get together socially and have fun – it helps with communication</li></ul>	<ul><li>Worry if the team does not work perfectly – it will need "fine tuning" from time to time</li><li>Let your team be "over-managed" so that members are not involved in decision making</li><li>Allow the team to become an "elite club" that doesn't work with other parts of the business</li><li>Miss any chance to congratulate the team on its successes</li><li>Let a "blame culture" develop – share responsibility when things go wrong</li></ul>

122

Now test your own team to see if you are winners - complete the next activity.

Are you part of a winning team?

	Answer these questions about your team as honestly as possible.	Yes	No
1	My team has ten members or less	☐	☐
2	I know the name of the team leader	☐	☐
3	My own team responsibilities are clear to me	☐	☐
4	I know well the responsibilities of the other team members	☐	☐
5	We are all clear about the overall team objectives	☐	☐
6	We always try to help each other in the team	☐	☐
7	When something goes wrong we can get another team member or the team leader to help	☐	☐
8	We have regular, well organised team meetings	☐	☐
9	When we have a real success, the whole team and others in the organisation get to hear about it	☐	☐
10	We regularly try to improve the team's service to customers	☐	☐
11	Every team member gets the chance to develop new skills or to do training	☐	☐
12	I enjoy working as a part of my team	☐	☐

Scoring Guideline	Add up your total score. Score 1 for Yes and 0 for No.
0 to 5 :	Your team needs sorting! Talk to your colleagues and manager about an urgent team improvement plan. You are letting your customers down at the moment.
6 to 9 :	Your team is working well, but there are some gaps. You may be losing some customers. Hold a team meeting and agree an improvement plan.
10 to 12 :	Perfection? Not quite! You can still improve, but your team is working hard to delight your customers.

123

6.7 Self-assessment

Module 6 Self-assessment

In each case tick the answer that best fits the question.

1	At work we nearly all work in:	Isolation from others	A	☐
		One large team	B	☐
		Teams	C	☐
2	Teams work best if they:	Communicate only when necessary	A	☐
		Work closely together	B	☐
		Have a powerful team leader	C	☐
3	Everyone in a team should know:	Everyone else's business	A	☐
		The job description of the manager	B	☐
		The roles of themselves and other team members	C	☐
4	Teams often work well if they have:	Charismatic leaders	A	☐
		A shared vision or purpose	B	☐
		More than 50 members	C	☐
5	Team meetings are a good way of:	Keeping everyone involved and informed	A	☐
		Dealing with customer complaints	B	☐
		Working out job roles	C	☐

6.8 Learning log

Now complete your learning log.

Learning log for Module 6

Add items to your learning log. When you get to the end of the programme you will need to refine these items to produce a clear action plan.

What I have learned
1
2
3
4
5

Actions planned	Target date
1	
2	
3	
4	
5	

Module summary

- Well done – in this module you have learned about the importance of team working for yourself, your customers (internal and external) and partner organisations. You are clear about the benefits of effective teams. You have analysed a team of which you are a member, and identified what you and your colleagues can do to improve its performance.

126

Module 7: Systems for delivering service excellence

Module introduction

Welcome to Module 7 of the Best Practice Guide for Customer Service Professionals. In this module you will learn how to focus on the processes you use with your customers, meeting their preferences and dealing with difficulties and problems. You will also see how the best organisations can use both product and service innovations to continually go the extra mile for their customers. Sections on service recovery and using Information and Communications Technology (ICT) to the benefit of staff and customers conclude the Module.

127

7.1 Learning outcomes

When you have successfully read through all the explanations and completed all the activities in this module you will be able to:

- Explain the importance of systems and procedures supporting consistent delivery of customer service
- Demonstrate an understanding that systems should be focused on customers
- Identify customer preferences and match them to available options
- Understand the meaning and benefits of product and service innovation
- Explain how organisations can benefit from customer feedback, both positive and negative
- Describe a systematic approach to service recovery
- Identify effective ways of resolving customers' problems
- Deal effectively with difficult customers and difficult customer service situations
- Understand the importance of using ICT to support systems and customers

7.2 Effective systems for customers

To provide service excellence you need to understand customers' needs. You must be skilled at communicating with them. You should be innovative in delivering "something extra" or "going the extra mile". (You must check what your organisation allows you to do first). However, even if you do all these things you will not delight all your customers unless you have effective systems. Systems guide you and your colleagues to deal with customers in the right way.

An organisation might decide to introduce or improve systems for any of the following reasons:

- To ensure that different staff all deal with customers in the same way
- Because complaints and problems are not always resolved properly
- Because customers have complained about they way they have been treated
- So that staff can take over from colleagues who are off sick, on holiday or leaving
- So that managers can monitor and control how customer service is being delivered

In most organisations there will be many different systems. They need to work well on their own and together. You will require good systems that do the following:

- Provide customers (and potential customers) with good information on your products and services
- Show and/or demonstrate to customers the products and services that you offer
- Enable customers to buy or access your products and services
- Obtain feedback from customers to find out what they think of your products and services
- Enable and encourage your customers to complain if they have a problem with your products and services
- Provide after-sale services to your customers
- Enable your organisation to make changes, innovations and improvements to your products and services

Examples of customer service systems include:
- Dealing with complaints
- Taking sales orders
- Recording transactions
- Responding to feedback
- Logging conversations and planned actions

7.3 The benefits of customer service procedures

Let us look in more detail at customer service systems. Systems are usually thought to be made up from a number of processes or procedures.

Definition Customer Service Procedures	Customer service procedures are the routines and detailed steps an organisation uses to deliver its customer service.

As an example, you may have a system for complaint handling. Within that system you will have a procedure for keeping a log of when the complaint was made, how it was dealt with, and finally how and when it was resolved. The key is that the whole system must work well for your customers and for you. (A system which works for you but not for the customer is not a good system).

A system which works for you but not for the customer is not a good system

Quote from ...	"We will ensure our procedures are customer friendly and easy for the customer and staff." (Johnston, 2003)
Shangri-La	

We shall look now at the benefits of having effective systems and procedures.

Staff understanding

Procedures help staff to understand how to deal with a particular aspect of their work with customers. They get used to using the procedure. After a while they become very familiar with the procedure, and so they can carry it out "automatically" without having to find out what to do. Some organisations document their procedures. They have written instructions on how to carry out the procedures, or flowcharts that describe the procedures visually.

Customer expectations

Procedures help customers directly. Customers know what to expect, and how they will be dealt with when accessing the product or service.

Working to service standards

Well designed procedures for customer service enable you and your managers to keep track of the standard of service that you are giving your customers. If everyone follows the procedures you can be confident that the customers' requirements are being met. This will be true as long as the procedures have been well designed with customers in mind. They need to be customer-focussed systems.

Provision of staff training

Most procedures and systems need to be explained in detail to the staff that are responsible for implementing them. Staff need to be trained. This may happen in the first few weeks of employment when the staff are learning how to do the job. Alternatively, if new systems and procedures are developed (for example to improve customer service), a training session will need to be delivered to the relevant staff members.

Quote from ... the RAC	"Employees don't fix cars, they fix people." (Johnston, 2003)

Quote from ... Shangri-La	"We will make customer satisfaction a key driver of our business." (Johnston, 2003)

Staff need to be trained

Quote from ... Tesco	"Be energetic, be innovative and be first for customers." (Johnston, 2003)

You should look at the procedures you use to see whether they can be improved to the benefit of customers. Do that with your own organisation by completing the next activity.

Activity

Making systems customer-focussed

Pick a system or procedure in your organisation that affects customer service. Try to think of a way of improving the system (from the point of view of the customer, rather than you). Then describe briefly what training would be needed to ensure that you and your colleagues implement the procedures correctly.

System improvement:

Training needed:

7.4 Identify and meet customer preferences

You need a system to make sure you are meeting your customers' preferences. In most organisations it is not enough simply to provide the product or service in the vain hope that it matches the customers' needs. Customers' needs change. In a competitive market other organisations will be looking to find new ways of winning customers from you. Your organisation must be responsive and alert to these changes. Therefore you do need a systematic way of checking what your customers want, and then providing it.

There are four key procedures here to include in your systems:

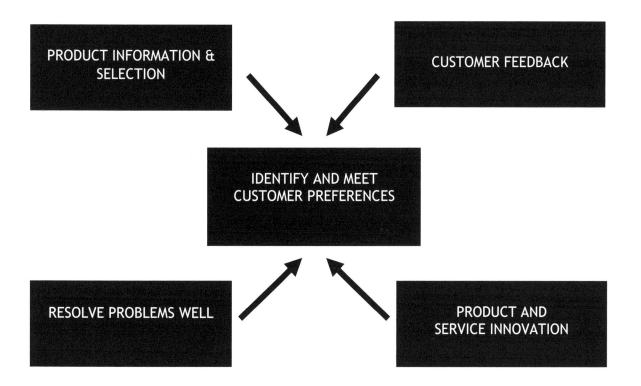

7.5 Product information and selection

Customers come to your organisation with the intention of doing business with you. They want to access your products or services – but which ones? Some organisations have a wide range to choose from, while for others the customers' choices will be simple. It depends on your particular business. At the very least you should be aware of the need to provide clear, effective information to your customers. Encourage them to make a good choice. Provide excellent service at this first stage of the customer relationship.

You should try to use a procedure which offers information on the full range of your products and services, so that the customer can make an effective choice.

to rely on product innovation alone. They must use service innovation. The task is to come up with new and radical levels of customer service in order to stand out from the rest.

Service innovation

Service innovation can be used to keep existing customers loyal and to attract new ones. The old days of 'If it ain't broke, don't fix it' are gone. Constant re-invention is how to stay ahead of customers. "Strong service companies survive the ups and downs of the market through the same means as fast-moving consumer goods like Gillette's. Brands like Harley-Davidson, IBM, Sears, Continental and American Express have all re-invented themselves at one point or other", says Shaun Smith (Smith, 2002). "This is not simply in order to follow the dictates of fashion, but to keep in front of changing consumer tastes". Better service can really delight the customer, even more than a change in the product itself. Also, service innovations can be quick and easy to implement.

136

Definition	Service innovation is the process of including new aspects of customer service along with the basic product or service. The new aspects are not provided by other organisations in the market, and so are likely to win over and keep new customers.
Service Innovation	

Case Study : Service Innovation

Look at this fictitious case study. Discuss how something similar might be used on your own organisation.

Service innovation in a Dental Practice

The staff of a dental practice wanted to improve the reputation of the business in order to win and keep more customers. The quality of the dental treatment provided had already been reviewed, and was of a very good standard.

The staff decided to implement a service innovation. They telephoned patients following stressful courses of treatment to ask how well they were recovering. Help, advice, further consultation and treatment was offered to patients who still had problems. This follow-up only took half an hour each day for one person to do. But word spread quickly in the area that this surprising service was given, and the dental practice soon increased its customer base.

137

The next activity looks at product and service innovation. Try to think of some product and service innovations for your own organisation (or one that you are familiar with).

138

Activity

Product innovation

Think of your own organisation or one that you are familiar with. Write below three ways in which product innovation is (or could be) used to make the products of the business more attractive than others in the market.

1	
2	
3	

Service innovation

Now move onto services. Write below three ways in which service innovation is (or could be) used to attract customers away from competitors.

1	
2	
3	

7.7 Systems for customer feedback

You need systems for getting feedback from your customers. The systems will allow you to check with the customer after choosing the product or service to find out how satisfied they are with that choice.

Definition	Customer feedback is information about customer perceptions of customer service collected by the organisation.
Customer Feedback	

Feedback from customers is important in order to:

- Find out whether services and products need to be improved
- Monitor the performance of the organisation
- Enable the organisation to respond to changes in customers' expectations

In the next activity you will identify a number of different ways of gaining this valuable feedback.

Activity

Listen to your customers

You must listen to your customers. Think of different ways that you could do this. Write down up to eight ways of listening to customers.

1	
2	
3	
4	
5	
6	
7	
8	

Use feedback to help you, your colleagues and your manager review the effectiveness of your customer service transactions. They are often moments of truth, so it is vital to regularly reflect on how well you are handling your customers and how you could improve. This is both a team issue and an individual one. Have regular team meetings and talk about problems and successes with customers. Get into the habit of making continual improvements to your own skills and procedures.

7.8   Resolve problems well – Six steps to service recovery

Dealing with complaints and resolving problems well is another key element of service excellence. You need to adopt a systematic approach to these kinds of situations.

Quote from ... Singapore Airlines	"Every passenger is important to us. We are there to try to help them." (Johnston, 2003)

Definition Service Recovery	Service recovery is a procedure for dealing with customers' problems and complaints. An effective service recovery procedure will turn a complaining customer into a satisfied, loyal customer.

The next activity gives some facts and figures about complaints.

Facts about complaints

Study these statistics on complaints.

- 90% of customers are likely to re-purchase from a company that has handled a complaint well
  (Hicks, 2003)

- 89% of customers are likely to tell others about a bad experience with a company
  (Hicks, 2006)

- 64% of customers expect a complaint to be dealt with immediately or on the same day; 86% of customers expect a written complaint to be resolved within one week
  (James, 2006)

- 52% of customers believe that UK companies are getting worse at handling complaints
  (Hicks, 2006)

Now write some brief ideas on what these fact and figures mean for you, your job and your organisation.

Resolving problems is not always easy, but it can be rewarding if you get it right and turn your customer into a loyal ambassador for your organisation. Complete the next activity.

Resolve problems well

Think back to a recent problem that one of your customers had. It might be a small one, which was easily resolved, or it could be something more serious.

What was the problem?	
What caused it?	
How did you respond?	
Did you respond in the best way? (Be honest)	
How will you react next time this happens?	
Were you able to resolve the problem yourself?	
Who did you report the problem to?	
How can the organisation as a whole reduce the chances of this problem occurring in the future?	
Do you have a system for how to deal with problems?	

Did you respond in the best way?

Value your complaints

If a customer complains and you fix the problem they are likely to stay loyal to you (and your organisation) more than someone who defects and has not complained. So the complaint is actually an excellent opportunity for you to win the loyalty of another customer! Also, you will gain valuable information about how to improve your service from the point of view of the customer. Look at the complaint as a positive opportunity.

Six steps to service recovery

Here is your framework for handling complaints and problems. It is useful for you to have a framework - a systematic approach to make sure you deal with the complaint in the right way. After all when someone does make a complaint it can be stressful to deal with. You may be worried that it is your fault. Or you might become involved with the customer's own emotions, especially if he or she is angry or upset. So use this framework, but do not be too rigid. Your task is to listen and empathise with your customer and do the very best that you can to help get over the situation.

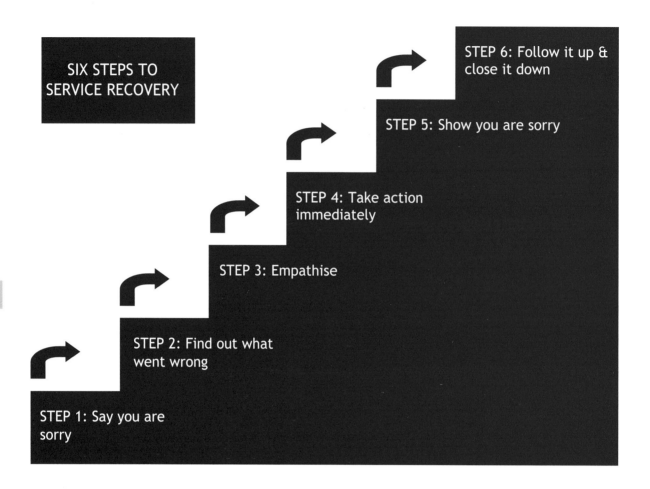

SIX STEPS TO SERVICE RECOVERY

STEP 6: Follow it up & close it down

STEP 5: Show you are sorry

STEP 4: Take action immediately

STEP 3: Empathise

STEP 2: Find out what went wrong

STEP 1: Say you are sorry

Step 1: Say you are sorry

Apologise sincerely. Make sure that it is you personally who is apologising to the customer. This can avert upset and anger, and, if you make it personal rather than a formal apology on behalf of "the company", it will be much better received. After all, the customer is looking to you individually to make amends and sort out the problem – the last thing they want is to deal with a faceless organisation. Customers know that it is people rather than organisations who can sort things out when they go wrong. When you make the apology, you do not need to admit or deny any responsibility or blame. Just see it from the customer's point of view and let them know that you can understand the problem they are having.

Step 2: Find out what went wrong

Ask the right questions in a sympathetic way to find out the nature of the problem. It may take some digging to get to the root of the problem. (Use your active listening skills – these were covered in section 5.7: Active listening skills). You may have to talk to colleagues, managers or other organisations to complete your fact-finding. If possible get more than one view of the facts, so that you can cross check and confirm that what was said is true.

Step 3: Empathise

Empathy is the ability to share in another's emotions or feelings. Try to feel the situation from your customer's point of view. Statements such as: "I can appreciate how you feel", "You're right", "It shouldn't have happened that way to you", all convey your empathy for the customer.

Step 4: Take action immediately

Next, convince your customer, quickly, that you are going to take action straight away to sort things out. The customer may be thinking: "Will anyone actually do anything to help me out, or will I just receive a meaningless apology?" An apology on its own is useless. You must be decisive and either set into motion a recovery plan or, if you really are unable to deal with the problem yourself, refer it to another, named person who you are confident can sort it out. Do not be tempted to pass the buck - if you can solve the problem yourself, do so. By all means get others involved, but remember that the customer is looking to you for the solution.

If you can recover the situation very quickly, say so, and make sure you do it. If it will take longer, say so and set into motion the recovery plan. Tell the customer exactly what will happen next.

Step 5: Show you are sorry

You need to convince the customer that you (on behalf of your organisation) are genuinely sorry - if a mistake has occurred. You will use your skills of communicating and empathy to do this. A customer will only be convinced that you are sorry when you have solved the problem and changed things so that it does not happen again. In most cases showing you are sorry stops there.

However, if the problem was a serious one, and there is a danger of losing the long term relationship with the customer, you may be empowered to give your customer some sort of symbol or gesture that says "I'm sorry". This depends on your organisation's policy, and on your manager. It is really a balance between the cost of losing the customer forever and the cost of providing the gift.

If you do this make sure you check with your manager first. In fact it is likely to be your manager who is empowered to decide whether a gift is appropriate. The gift could be anything - money, a voucher, flowers, an apology letter, or anything else which sends the right message to the customer. In a hotel it could be an extra night's accommodation. An airline might give a free upgrade.

Step 6: Follow it up and close it down

Follow-up is essential. Complete the job. Do what you said you would do (and more if possible). If you deal with a lot of complaints or problems, make a habit of always checking to see if there are outstanding issues to deal with.

146

Use a system. Your organisation may have computer software, which flags up outstanding complaints. Try to use this effectively. Reduce your closedown times as much as you can. If there are (organisational) reasons why complaints are not getting closed down quickly enough, discuss the issue with your colleagues and supervisor. You may be able to keep a lot more customers loyal if you can change the system to reduce the closedown times.

7.9 Handling difficult customers by staying positive

If you deal with customers then at some stage you will almost certainly have to deal with a difficult situation. How you handle difficult customers is important. Be positive. Stay calm. Try to act smartly to turn a difficult customer into a loyal one (but accept that this is not always possible).

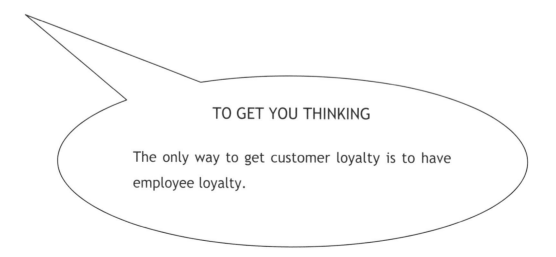

TO GET YOU THINKING

The only way to get customer loyalty is to have employee loyalty.

Use positive language to turn difficult situations into good ones. Tell customers what you can do rather than what you can't do. To use positive language you need to concentrate on how you communicate. With positive communication, you don't blame people - you solve problems. There is always a way to talk positively rather than negatively – and if you do this you will find that your difficult customers become easier to talk to. Try this out by completing the next activity.

TOP TIP

When you are dealing with an aggressive customer on the telephone try standing up! You will feel more in control of the situation.

Use positive language

Turn the following negative statements into positive statements by using positive language. There are some for external customers and some for internal customers. There is an example to start you off.

Negative statement	Positive statement
Negative statement	Example positive statement
"You didn't complete the form properly."	"Let me help you with this so we can get it processed straight away."

External customers

Negative statement	Positive statement
"We are short staffed so we can't deal with everyone straight away."	
"Don't you realise you are talking to the wrong department about this?"	
"You should have 'phoned earlier. We are just about to close."	
"I can't deal with your repair unless you give me the serial number."	

Internal customers

Negative statement	Positive statement
"I'm too busy to answer your questions now."	
"You don't need to know that. Just get on with your job and I'll do mine."	
"Can't you get this information to me more quickly? I need it earlier in the month."	
"That's not my job. Try the finance section."	

7.10 Handling conflict Dos and Don'ts

Occasionally you may have to deal with a really difficult situation. This could involve either internal customers or external customers. To be prepared for these situations keep in mind the following Dos and Don'ts.

Handling conflict Dos and Don'ts	
Do:	Don't:
Tackle conflict early, to avoid it escalating	Take it personally, it is a fact of life
Think it through and plan how to deal with the conflict	Avoid the issue and ignore the conflict
Refrain from offering your own opinion before understanding the full picture	Fight anger with anger
Try to avoid instinctive reactions	Jump in without assessing and understanding the problem
Stay assertive	Run away

149

7.11 Use ICT to support your systems

Information and Communications Technology (ICT) gives you a great opportunity to develop effective systems for customer service. The best IT systems are ones that are simple, and designed around customers. Use ICT to support your customers.

Systems that are simple and easy to use and understand can help provide consistent service. They store important information about customers. This will help you work with the right customers and give them great customer service.

Systems can provide a platform from which to plan service recovery. Research about customers' views of technology shows that:

- Customers' expectations are increasing

- Customers will no longer tolerate frequent faults with ICT - fractured service, failed service promises, discrimination, poorly trained and de-motivated staff
- Customers are clear about what they want from technology - a choice of human and technology channels
- Customers want technology to improve the service they receive

Customer service information

It is important to use ICT systems effectively. Get to know the software and the hardware and how to use them. If your skills are lacking, ask for training or coaching. (Coaching could be given one-to-one, while you are carrying out your normal work).

150

When you deal with your customer you will be collecting information about them. Remember to keep to your organisation's guidelines for data protection – this is covered in section 8.4: Data Protection and Freedom of Information.

Accurate and timely data

When you collect information make sure you take the time and trouble to ensure it is accurate. You may need to ask questions of your customers if some information is missing. The more accurate you are, the better will be the service you provide. Collect the information – and record it – at the time you are supposed to and in the time you are given. It can be tempting to leave some information until later, but this may cause a gap in the records that are need by your colleagues – your internal customers. Be methodical when dealing with customer information, checking and validating information wherever you can.

Here are some examples of ICT systems you might use to help you deliver excellent customer service:

- Maintaining a database of customer information
- Keeping records of customer transactions
- Using email to communicate with customers
- Using websites for sales orders, order tracking and products catalogues 24 hours a day

Here are your Dos and Don'ts for systems:

Systems Dos and Don'ts

Do:	Don't:
• Keep ICT systems simple • Use systems to support people, both staff and customers • Use the technology to help make your business easier for the customer • Assess how a change in one part of the system will affect other parts • Be accurate and timely in your collection of customer information • Ask for help if your ICT skills need to be improved	• Lose the personal touch by allowing yourself to become remote from the customer • Let the systems you use be management focused – they should be customer focused • Let technology get in the way of using systems to help people • Rush to complete transactions – without ensuring all your required information is there • Ignore your organisations data protection policy and guidelines

Keep systems simple

7.12 Self-assessment

		Module 7 Self-assessment		
		In each case tick the answer that best fits the question.		
1	Systems should be:	Focused on the cost	A	☐
		Focused on the customer	B	☐
		Focused on the regulations	C	☐
2	Customer service procedures are:	The routines needed to deliver customer service	A	☐
		The methods of taking telephone calls	B	☐
		Legal requirements	C	☐
3	A system which works for you but not for the customer is:	The most effective type of system	A	☐
		Not a good system	B	☐
		Customer focused	C	☐
4	If you are not sure how to use a process or procedure you should:	Ask a colleague or manager for guidance	A	☐
		Book to go on an external training course	B	☐
		Just carry on and try your best	C	☐
5	When trying to meet your customers' preferences you should:	Emphasise the products you have in stock	A	☐
		Emphasise the features rather than the benefits	B	☐
		Emphasise the benefits rather than the features	C	☐

7.13 Learning log

Now complete your learning log.

Activity

Learning log for Module 7

Add items to your learning log. When you get to the end of the programme you will need to refine these items to produce a clear action plan.

What I have learned
1
2
3
4
5

Actions planned	Target date
1	
2	
3	
4	
5	

153

Module summary

- Well done – in this module you have learned about systems and the need to keep them as simple and as customer focused as possible. Gaining feedback is vital to meeting the preferences of your customers. Handling difficult situations is best done by staying as positive as you can, and it is recommended that you adopt a step-by-step checklist approach when you deal with complaints. ICT systems should be reviewed to make sure they help you, your colleagues and your customers. Be prepared to recommend changes to systems and to think of new, better versions of your products and services so that you can keep your customers delighted.

154

Module 8: Laws and codes of practice

Module introduction

Welcome to Module 8 of the Best Practice Guide for Customer Service Professionals. In this module you will learn about some of the key laws that are likely to affect your customer service roles and responsibilities. We will also refer to codes of practice – those guidelines that apply to particular sectors.

8.1 Learning outcomes

155

When you have successfully read through all the explanations and completed all the activities in this module you will be able to:

- Understand the main aspects of customer service that are affected by legislation, regulation and sector codes of practice

- Recognise the main regulatory and legal restrictions on what you can and cannot do in all aspects of your work with customers

8.2 Laws and regulations - how they affect you

What you can and cannot do in your customer service role is important. There are laws and regulations that control how you act. It is up to you to make sure you keep to them. They are there to guide you. If you do not keep them you will get yourself and your organisation into difficulty.

Find out about the different levels of laws and regulations that affect what you do in your job:

- Laws
- Regulations
- Sector guide-lines or codes of practice
- Organisational policies and procedures

Make sure you find out all you can. Check your organisation's policies and procedures - these might be in an employee handbook. Recall the information you were given when you first started your job – perhaps in an induction pack. Talk to your colleagues and manager about the aspects that you are unsure of. Finally, use the websites at the end of this module to check on the legal issues and guidelines that affect the way you do your job.

8.3 Consumer laws for customers' rights

Advertising goods

You should be aware that if goods or services are advertised, or even if you describe them verbally to a customer, then the customer has certain legal rights. Advertising must not be misleading and must not be in breach of the Trades Description Act. Goods should correspond with the description you give, whether it's verbally or in writing. It is an offence under the Trade Descriptions Act to describe goods misleadingly.

156

Selling goods

The goods you sell must be "of suitable quality" and be "fit for the purpose for which they are sold." If people buy a pen, for instance, it must be capable of writing. But this requirement also means that if a customer tells you they want an item for a particular purpose, you should tell them if you have doubts about its suitability.
Goods must be of "satisfactory quality." They must be durable, safe and free from defects. If goods don't meet these criteria, your customers can claim a refund if they haven't already "accepted" them. (Customers accept goods if they tell you they've accepted them, alter the goods or keep them for a reasonable length of time).

Breaking the Sale and Supply of Goods Act (1979) gives the customer rights to damages, money back or a replacement, depending upon the circumstances. Customers cannot reject goods simply because they've changed their mind.   They cannot claim a refund after accepting goods, but they could claim compensation. This can be monetary but could be the repair or replacement of goods. If your customer is an individual rather than another business they can specify that they want either a repair or a replacement. There may also be safety standards for the goods. If you ignore these your organisation could be liable to criminal prosecution and face a large claim for damages.

Food sales must comply with the terms of the Food & Drugs Act. For advice on this law you or someone in your organisation could contact the local health department, the local Trading Standards Office or The Office of Fair Trading in London. Food and drink sales must also comply with the Weights & Measures Act. For information on this contact the Trading Standards Office.

If goods are sold on instalment or credit basis then the Credit Act applies. The business must be registered under the Act first.

The Consumer Protection (Distance Selling) Regulations (2000) will apply if you sell goods to customers by telephone or on-line. If you are selling goods you have to provide consumers with certain information and give them a 7 working day cooling off period.

Selling Services

There may be restrictions on particular services. For example, lawyers and accountants have strict conduct rules to consider and estate agents have some conduct rules. Your organisation should inform you of these rules.

If you give advice to people, your organisation should have taken out professional indemnity insurance in case someone sues you for giving bad advice.

Find out how these laws and other regulations apply to your own organisation (or one that you are familiar with). Think carefully about what you should do in your customer service role. Check if the organisation has policies that refer to these laws. Ask a manager - or a Human Resource or Personnel representative – to help you with your research.

Activity

Consumer laws:
Implications for the customer service professional

Find out how your organisation is affected by Consumer Laws. Make brief notes below on what you will need to do to comply with the laws.

8.4 Data Protection and Freedom of Information

Data Protection Act

The Data Protection Act is designed to protect personal information – that is, information about individual people. Even the telephone number of a customer is personal information. The act does not apply to commercial information unless personal data is also involved.

Information about people, whether it is held on computer or on paper, must be kept safe and secure. As soon as you record some personal information, on computer or on paper, you are taking a risk. That information may be lost, corrupted or even accessed by somebody and misused, and that is illegal. Respect the confidentiality of your customers by keeping to your organisation's procedures and the Data Protection Act.

Data Protection Principles

The Data Protection Act refers to Data Subjects and Data Users. To be clear on who these people are:

- The Data Subject is the person whose personal data is held on file
- The Data User is the organisation that holds the personal data on file

There are eight principles in the Data Protection Act (1998). They are:

1. Data which is held must be fairly and lawfully obtained and processed. Data files must be registered (like registering a car or the birth of a child).
2. Personal data must only be used for limited purposes. Those purposes must be stated when the data file is registered.
3. The data held about people must only be what is needed for the registered purposes – it must be "adequate, relevant and not excessive."
4. The organisation that holds the personal data must ensure that it is accurate and true.
5. Personal data must not be kept for longer than is necessary (for the purposes stated).
6. Personal Data must be processed in line with the data subject's rights.
7. Personal Data must be kept secure (So that, for example, no-one else can access it and potentially misuse it).
8. Personal Data must not be transferred to other countries without adequate protection.

By law, Data Users must keep to the eight principles. As Data Subjects we all have the right to request a printed copy of our record. If we want to do this, we need to find out the details of the Data User. If we find that the data is wrong, we can insist that the Data User corrects it, or else removes it from their records.

To keep to the Data Protection Act, follow the guidelines in your list of Dos and Don'ts.

Data Protection Dos and Don'ts	
Do:	**Don't:**
• Check your organisation's procedures • Keep to the organisation's guidelines on how to collect, store and retrieve information about your customers • Keep to the eight Data Protection Principles • Use computer identities and passwords properly to protected personal data from misuse by unauthorised people • Check with your manager before you change the type of customer information that you record	• Keep a permanent record about an individual customer if you don't need to - that record may be open to loss, corruption or misuse • Keep information about individual customers except in a personal data file that has been registered • Pass customer information onto others unless you know that this is allowed under the Data Protection Act

159

Freedom of Information Act

This Act applies to public authorities, such as:

• government departments

• local authorities

• educational establishments

• NHS GPs and dentists

• police forces

• health authorities

The Freedom of Information Act (2000) gives people the right of access to information held by or on behalf of public authorities. Its aim is to create better public understanding of:

• how public authorities carry out their duties

• why they make their decisions

- how they spend public money

What sort of information can be accessed?

The Freedom of Information Act gives the right of access to all recorded information held by public authorities. It can be held in documents, emails, notes, videos, letters and even audio tapes. The information does not have to be about the person requesting it, and a reason for wanting it does not have to be given.

If your work is in a public authority you should check to find out your organisation's policy on Freedom of Information. Be aware of what you can and cannot record in your customer service role.

160

Requesting the information

There are two ways to ask for the information held by a public authority.

You can make a formal freedom of information request. This must:

- be in writing
- clearly describe the information you want
- include your name and address

Publication schemes

Alternatively every public authority makes some information publicly available already. It should describe this information in a 'publication scheme'. The scheme will often be posted on the public authority's website.

If the requested information is covered by a publication scheme, the public authority should provide it without delay. However, if someone makes a formal freedom of information request, a public authority has up to 20 days to decide whether the law permits the person to have the information. In some cases this time limit may be extended. If so, the public authority should write to say when it will be able to send the information.

Charges for information

The Information Commissioner expects that public authorities should provide as much information as possible free of charge. If charges are made – for example the information might have been produced for sale – the charges should be reasonable.

Exemptions

There are some exemptions to the act, so that public authorities can withhold information that should not be released into the public domain. Examples include information that might identify other people or compromise national security. If a public authority intends to rely on an exemption to withhold information, it must send a refusal notice stating the exemption and saying why it applies.

Find out how the law and other regulations apply to your own organisation (or one that you are familiar with). Think carefully about what you should do in your customer service role. Check if the organisation has policies that refer to these laws. Ask a manager - or a Human Resource or Personnel representative – to help you with your research.

Activity

Data Protection and Freedom of Information: Implications for the customer service professional

Find out how your organisation is affected by the Data Protection and Freedom of Information Acts. Make brief notes below on what you will need to do to comply with the law.

8.5 Sex Discrimination Act (1975)

The Sex Discrimination Act 1975 (SDA) prohibits sex discrimination against individuals in the areas of employment, education, and the provision of goods, facilities and services and in the disposal or management of premises. It also prohibits discrimination in employment against married people. Victimisation because someone has tried to exercise their rights under the SDA is prohibited.

The SDA applies to women and men of any age, including children. Discriminatory advertisements are unlawful but only the Equal Opportunities Commission can take action against advertisers. There are some general exceptions to when sex discrimination is unlawful. The main exceptions are:

- When a charity is providing a benefit to one sex only, in accordance with its charitable instrument
- When people are competing in a sport in which the average woman is at a disadvantage to the average man because of physical strength, stamina or physique
- In insurance where the discriminatory treatment reasonably relates to actuarial or other data

162

Find out how these laws and other regulations apply to your own organisation (or one that you are familiar with). Think carefully about what you should do in your customer service role. Check if the organisation has policies that refer to these laws. Ask a manager - or a Human Resource or Personnel representative – to help you with your research.

Activity

**Sex discrimination:
Implications for the customer service professional**

Find out how your organisation is affected by sex discrimination issues. Make brief notes below on what you will need to do to comply with the law.

TO GET YOU THINKING

What facilities and services does your organisation provide for customers with specific needs? Can you improve?

8.6 Disability Discrimination Act (DDA)

Definition of Disability under the terms of the DDA

Under the DDA of 1995, a person is considered to be disabled if he or she has a physical or mental impairment which has a substantial and long-term adverse effect on their ability to carry out normal day-to-day activities. The disability is to have lasted or be likely to last 12 months or over. People who have had a disability within the definition are protected from discrimination even if they are no longer disabled.

Employers with 15 or more employees must not discriminate against current or prospective employees who have, or have had a disability. Disabilities may relate to:

- Learning difficulties
- Visual, hearing or speaking impairments
- Physical handicaps

Employers have a duty to make reasonable adjustments, at all stages of the employment process, where physical features of their premises or arrangements place a disabled person at a substantial disadvantage to a non-disabled person.

It is important that you understand the meaning of the word "reasonable" in the DDA. Organisations are expected to make "reasonable" adjustments so that disabled people can access their products and services. However, the DDA is not about putting organisations out of business. Adjustments for disabled people can often be made at little or no cost or disruption – so an organisation should make these adjustments.

As just one example, many products and services are now offered via websites. Your organisation's website can quite easily be adjusted so that people with visual impairment will find it possible, or easier, to use. Tim Berners-Lee, the inventor of the World Wide Web, once said: "The power of the Web is in its universality. Access by everyone regardless of disability is an essential aspect." Under the DDA, websites should be user friendly for disabled people. The World Wide Web Consortium (WC3) has recognised the need for universal accessibility and has published some Web Content Accessibility Guidelines to reduce potential difficulties. These are voluntary guidelines, but can help an organisation using the web to check on how it can improve accessibility for its disabled customers.

Changes to the physical structure of buildings might be needed. These tend to be expensive, but the organisation should make every effort to find other ways of meeting the needs of disabled people. They should not be disadvantaged compared to non-disabled people. It may be, for example, that next time the organisation goes through a major change or re-structure, the location of areas that disabled customers use can be re-sited.

Find out how these laws and other regulations apply to your own organisation (or one that you are familiar with). Think carefully about what you should do in your customer service role. Check if the organisation has policies that refer to these laws. Ask a manager - or a Human Resource or Personnel representative – to help you with your research.

Activity

Disability Discrimination Act: Implications for the customer service professional

Find out how your organisation is affected by the Disability Discrimination Act. Make brief notes below on what you will need to do to comply with the law.

8.7 Health and Safety at Work Act

Under the Health and Safety at Work Act your organisation must ensure the health and safety of yourself, your colleagues and your customers. They are all affected by what you do or fail to do.

This law applies to people who:

- Are employed by your organisation (including casual workers, part time workers, trainees and subcontractors)
- Use your organisation's workplaces
- Are allowed to use your organisation's work equipment
- Visit your premises – including customers
- May be affected by your work - for example neighbours or the public
- Use products you make, supply or import – again applying to your customers
- Use your professional services, for example if your organisation offers a design service

Everyone has a "duty of care" to those who may be affected by their actions. A duty of care means that you must take all reasonable steps to ensure the safety of any person that you deal with.

Your organisation has a duty to take reasonable care of the workforce by:

- Providing safe plant and machinery
- Ensuring you employ competent staff
- Providing safe systems of work

This affects you as a customer service professional in these ways:

- You owe a duty of care to your customers, people who you work alongside and members of the public.
- You should know your organisation's Health and Safety Policy, and how it applies to you as a customer service professional.
- For the area you work in a person should have been identified who will regularly carry out a health and safety risk assessment. This risk assessment tells you what you should do to safeguard yourself and other people and to comply with your legal duties.

165

- You must cooperate with any other business in the same premises on safety issues. For example, you might need to provide them with information on any safety risks, and having a joint fire evacuation plan.

Use the Health and Safety at Work Act to help you in your daily work with customers. Do not think of Health and Safety as something that someone else does – we are all responsible for it. There is probably a Health and Safety Officer where you work. Their job is to guide you to work safely. Read the risk assessments and take note of them. Think, whenever you are carrying out a new responsibility, about how you ensure the safety of all those you deal with.

For yourself, make sure you know:
- Your organisation's Health and Safety Policy and Procedures
- Who the Health and Safety Officer is
- Where the risk assessments that affect you are kept
- What the risk assessments tell you about how to work safely

For your customers, make sure you know:
- what might endanger them or their property
- the specific risks and hazards that could endanger your customers
- how they should avoid the risks and hazards

Working on customers' premises

You may work on your customer's premises. This could be an individual customer or an organisation. Whichever it is, make sure that you respect the feelings of individuals customers. Follow the procedures and guidelines of the customer as an organisation. Fit in with their Health and Safety procedures. Make certain that you look at and take note of any risk assessments that currently apply to the customer's premises or equipment. Plan - before you start work – what you will do if there is a problem.

Even if you are working at the property of an individual customer, make sure you respect the customer. Be aware of peoples' feelings and be sure to treat the customer and his or her property and possessions accordingly.

Dealing with accidents whilst working on customer's premises

When you are on a customer's premises, you should know in advance what to do if there is an accident or problem. What does the customer need to you to do and how does your own organisation want you to proceed? Find out before you go to the customer what insurance cover your own organisation has provided. If, for example, you damage your customer's property, your own organisation should have insurance cover to the right level so that claims can be made without any difficulty. Consider also your own, personal liability, and check that this is included in your organisation's insurance policy. Finally, certain you know what information to ask and record in the case of an accident, just as you would if you had a car accident.

Find out how these laws and other regulations apply to your own organisation (or one that you are familiar with). Think carefully about what you should do in your customer service role. Check if the organisation has policies that refer to these laws. Ask a manager - or a Human Resource or Personnel representative – to help you with your research.

167

Activity

Health and Safety at Work: Implications for the customer service professional

Find out how your organisation is affected by Health and Safety at Work issues. Make brief notes below on what you will need to do to comply with the law.

8.8 Human Rights Act and other EU legislation and directives

The Human Rights Act 1998 applies to all public authorities. It makes it unlawful for bodies like the police, government departments, and local councils etc. to violate the rights contained in the European Convention on Human Rights. The Human Rights Act consists of a number of "basic" rights and freedoms:

8.13 Self-assessment

Module 8 Self-assessment

In each case tick the answer that best fits the question.

1	Codes of practice are:	Guide-lines in your sector or industry	A	☐
		Legal requirements	B	☐
		Company procedures	C	☐
2	The Data Protection Act applies to:	Commercial information	A	☐
		Financial information	B	☐
		Personal information	C	☐
3	Health and Safety is the responsibility of:	Everyone at work	A	☐
		Only the Health and Safety Officer	B	☐
		Mainly your manager	C	☐
4	The Disability Discrimination Act applies to organisations that employ:	1 to 10 people	A	☐
		Disabled people	B	☐
		15 or more people	C	☐
5	The Freedom of Information Act applies to:	All organisations	A	☐
		Organisation employing more than 100 people	B	☐
		Public sector organisations	C	☐

8.14 Learning log

Now complete your learning log.

Activity

Learning log for Module 8

Add items to your learning log. When you get to the end of the programme you will need to refine these items to produce a clear action plan.

What I have learned
1
2
3
4
5

Actions planned	Target date
1	
2	
3	
4	
5	

177

Module summary

- Well done – in this module you have learned about the main laws that affect your customer service role. You have researched the actions that you can and cannot take relating to customers. You need to take careful note of two further sources of advice – firstly, the guidelines that your organisation produces and secondly any codes of practice that apply to all the organisations in your sector. Finally you will be aware of websites that can advise you about future changes to the laws and codes of practice that apply to your customer service role.

178

Module 9: The you factor

Module introduction

Welcome to Module 9 of the Best Practice Guide for Customer Service Professionals. In this module you will learn about emotional intelligence and its relevance to customer service. You will see that your own skills, attitudes and behaviour have a key effect on how you relate to others, including customers. You will be able to develop a plan for your own professional development which may fit with your organisation's procedures for appraisal and performance review.

179

9.1 Learning outcomes

When you have successfully read through all the explanations and completed all the activities in this module you will be able to:

- Identify the skills of emotional intelligence that are relevant to customer service
- Demonstrate an understanding of the effects of submissive, assertive and aggressive behaviours on others
- Understand how personal attitude, health and emotional state affect your ability to deliver excellent customer service
- Plan and carry out activities that are needed for your own professional development

Getting fit to be a customer service professional

This module is all about you. To deliver great service you need to get fit to be a customer service professional. But what is a customer service professional? Here is a simple definition:

Definition Customer Service Professional	A customer service professional is someone who is well equipped to understand and meet the customer's needs.

9.3 Emotional intelligence

Being aware of your own emotions and those of your customers is important. If you are emotionally intelligent you will be better prepared to listen to customers, exceed their expectations and deal with problems. Here is a definition:

Definition Emotional Intelligence	Emotional intelligence is understanding the emotions of yourself and your customers, and how they are likely to change in different situations.

Try to develop and use the five emotional intelligence competencies below.

Emotional intelligence competencies for customer service	
Stress tolerance	• Being able to get through stressful situations without "falling apart" or reacting in a negative way • Coping with stress in an active and positive way • Being optimistic about working through problems to overcome them
Assertiveness	• Expressing your thoughts and beliefs openly • Standing up for what you believe • Being prepared to stand up for what you believe without dismissing the beliefs of other people
Happiness	• Feeling satisfied with your own life and enjoying being with other people • Being cheerful and enthusiastic • Able to take positive action to deal with your own stress or problems
Interpersonal relationships	• Able to establish and maintain satisfying personal and professional relationships • Feeling comfortable in dealings with other people
Self-actualisation	• Recognising your own strengths and weaknesses • Being aware of where you need to improve your own skills and competencies • Having your own clear goals and a sense of purpose

Now try this simple self-assessment activity:

Activity

Emotional intelligence self-assessment

For each of the five emotional intelligence competencies, think about your own competency and give yourself a score out of ten.

Competency	Score out of ten
Stress tolerance	
Assertiveness	
Happiness	
Interpersonal relationships	
Self-actualisation	

Now pick the two competencies with the lowest scores.

For each one, note down your ideas on:

- How you could improve?
- Where could you get help to improve?
- Who could you ask for help?

181

9.4 Stress tolerance

Many of us suffer from stress from time to time. Some people say that stress is good for us, because it "keeps us on our toes" and helps us to do a good job. However, stress can get out of control and have a drastic effect on our lives and jobs.

Stress may come from the job or the personal life. If the stress comes from your home life, use success in your job to counteract it. If the stress comes from the job, use your personal life to do things which relieve the stress, such as exercise and leisure activities. The best reason for becoming a customer service professional could be the job satisfaction that you get from your customers – thereby reducing your stress levels.

182

9.5 Assertiveness

When you deal with customers they may behave in one of several distinctive ways. You yourself can also behave differently depending on the situation. To be assertive you should recognise your behaviour and that of your customers.

Peoples' behaviour towards each other may be:
- Submissive
- Assertive
- Aggressive

We shall look at each type of behaviour in turn.

Submissive behaviour

When you give in to the other person you are being submissive. You put other peoples' feelings and wants before your own. You might appear to be polite, but really you will not feel good about yourself.

Try to recognise these signs of submissive behaviour:
- Avoiding eye contact
- Fidgeting
- Always apologising
- Putting yourself down
- Agreeing to do what you do not want to do

- Speaking quietly and nervously

Submissive behaviour is like that of a child who is doing what he or she is told by an adult.

Assertive behaviour

Assertive behaviour, on the other hand, is adult. It involves thinking and reasoning. If you act assertively you put your own point across in a clear, firm, but fair manner. You act assertively to get what you want from a situation. However, true assertive behaviour involves valuing the opinions and rights of others. If you make your own points but ignore the rights and feelings of others then your behaviour becomes aggressive rather than assertive.

There are signs that indicate when someone is acting assertively. These may include:
- Clear and confident speech
- Stating what you want, think and feel
- Standing up for what you believe to be correct
- Listening to the other person and acknowledging their views
- Relaxed body posture and facial expression
- Being open and honest with the other person

Aggressive behaviour

This is when you disregard the feelings and views of others. You put your own wants before those of other people. Signs of aggressive behaviour are quite easy to spot. They may include:
- Speaking loudly or shouting
- Giving orders
- Finger wagging and pointing
- Interrupting others
- Putting others down
- Using sarcasm

183

184

Signs of aggressive behaviour are quite easy to spot

The best behaviour to use as a customer service professional is assertive behaviour. This is not always easy because you may have to deal with customers who act aggressively.

Here are some tips to help you to deal with aggressive customers:

Dealing with aggressive customers

You will sometimes find that your customers act aggressively towards you. Try to recognise the signs, but do not take it personally. Use assertive behaviour yourself, but do not fall into the trap of also being aggressive. If you do become aggressive this will almost certainly make the situation even worse – it will not solve the problem. Use the following tips to withstand the pressure.

- Be confident in your voice, facial expression and posture. If your body language is assertive your mind will probably soon follow.
- Ask the right questions to diffuse the situation.
- Be factual - do not be tempted to always express your own opinions or emotions.
- Work out how the situation can be taken forward and state clearly and calmly what you intend to do.
- Maintain eye contact with your customer but do not glare.
- If it helps and it is appropriate, apologise. However, do not simply admit blame on behalf of your organisation or other people just satisfy the aggressive customer - it could land you in trouble. In other words, do not be submissive.
- If the aggression of the customer goes beyond your ability to handle the situation, know when to get the help of others, such as your manager.
- At all times act professionally and calmly.

185

The vicious circle of behaviour

It is all too easy to "follow the customer's lead" and adopt their behaviour. This is especially true if a customer is rude and aggressive. The vicious circle of behaviour is shown below.

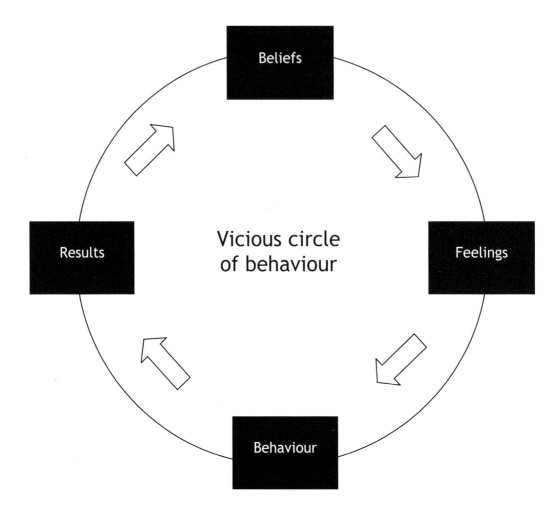

Look at how the vicious circle of behaviour works when you deal with a difficult customer. If your belief is simply that the customer is being rude, perhaps with no good reason, your feelings may turn to anger. If you are angry this in turn tends to make your own behaviour aggressive. The result is that the conversation will go from bad to worse.

As a customer service professional you need to recognise the behaviour of the customer, and try to break into the circle. How do you do this? What you must do is turn a negative into a positive. Adopt a positive interpretation. Break the circle between beliefs and feelings. Try to understand that the customer is acting aggressively due to specific reasons. Do not be concerned that these reasons are not good reasons. Use assertive behaviour and your own knowledge of the situation to turn your own feelings from anger to assertiveness.

This is a skill that you can learn. Once you have learned how to break into the vicious circle of behaviour and you have practised the technique several times you will be capable of dealing effectively with some very difficult situations.

Happiness through personal attitude and motivation

Your personal attitude affects the impression you give to your customers. The ideal attitude is to be totally positive, but this is not realistic. We cannot be happy all of the time. Be aware that if you bring problems in your personal life to work, your professionalism will suffer. There is no easy answer here, but try to stay professional at all times.

Your personal attitude affects the impression you give to your customers

Quote from ...	"We will create an environment where our people may achieve their personal and career goals." (Johnston, 2003)
Shangri-La	

External influences

You spend a lot of your life at work, and you will find that your work is rewarding if you do an excellent job. External influences, from outside of your work, will have an effect on your job. Problems might be:

- Family or relationship troubles

- Your own health problems

- Family or friends' health problems

- Money worries

- Changes such as moving home, getting married, separating or having children

- Caring for ill or elderly relatives

There are others but reduce the effects of these problems by making a conscious effort to deal with them. Do not just lie back and accept the difficulties of life. Try to minimise and deal with them. If you can do that, you may find that work improves also (with a more positive attitude) and your whole life can seem more "in control."

Some ways of dealing with such problems are:

- Keep healthy:
  - Don't smoke
  - Have a healthy, balanced diet
  - Exercise regularly
  - Have interests or hobbies, or just something different to do that can take your mind off the problems

- Talk to others about your problems – it helps to have someone just to listen

- If the problems become serious, make sure you consult with people who can help you

- Be decisive and change the things that are not working – get control of your life

9.7 Interpersonal relationships

Most of what you do at work involves other people. You do not generally choose the people you work with. However, the better you get on with these people, the better you will be able to do your job. Your effectiveness depends partly on the quality of the relationships you have.

Try to establish successful interpersonal relationships with:

- customers
- managers
- team members
- people in other departments
- people in other organisations (such as suppliers)

This does not been that you can expect to be the best of friends with everyone. Simply try to maintain a professional relationship with them all. Treat them as internal or external customers. Use your skills of emotional intelligence, especially assertiveness, to be aware of your behaviour, their behaviour, and how the two interact.

You need to feel confident in your dealings with the whole range of people at work. This is not always easy. For example, many people find that they are uncomfortable when speaking to their manager. It is common to revert to a child-adult mode of behaviour when you are with someone in authority. Review section 5.8: Use behaviour appropriate to the situation. This covers the child and adult ego states in transactional analysis. Change your mode of behaviour to adult in these situations. Use your techniques of assertiveness to establish a proper adult-adult relationship, where both people assert their own views but listen and respond to the other's views as well.

Another common problem is to find particular people at work difficult to get on with. You may feel that someone is awkward or unhelpful towards you. Some people are difficult to establish relationships with. The point is, you need to relate to them in a professional way, as customers, in order to get the job done. Again, be aware of how your own behaviour and responses will affect the relationship. Act as an adult. Be assertive. Do not fall into the trap of copying their behaviour. Act as a professional, be positive, and see whether this improves the relationship. Above all, do not take it personally. If you find some people difficult to deal with then others probably do as well. Regard it as a challenge!

Interpersonal relationships in your home life can have an effect on your working life. Many people have difficult times with their partners, relatives and friends from time to time. As a customer service professional try to reduce the overspill of your home life into your work. Again this is not necessarily easy. However, it is important that, for example, being unhappy in one part of your life does not adversely affect the other and make you even unhappier! Be positive, act as an adult and think carefully about what you can do to improve the situation. Emotional intelligence is not just something to use at work. Try out your techniques of assertiveness, adult behaviour and active listening skills on your friends and family.

Complete the following activity to check and improve your interpersonal relationships.

190

<table>
<tr><td colspan="6" align="right">Activity</td></tr>
<tr><td colspan="6">Check your interpersonal relationships</td></tr>
<tr><td colspan="6">Think about the some of your relationships at work and at home. Try to say whether each one is satisfactory or unsatisfactory. For each one decide whether the use of assertiveness skills, adult behaviour or active listening skills would improve the relationship. If you want, add some action points to your learning log action plan.</td></tr>
<tr><td></td><td></td><td></td><td colspan="3">Relationship could benefit from my use of:</td></tr>
<tr><td>Relationship</td><td>Satis-factory</td><td>Unsatis-factory</td><td>Assertive-ness skills</td><td>Adult behaviour</td><td>Active listening skills</td></tr>
<tr><td></td><td>☐</td><td>☐</td><td></td><td></td><td></td></tr>
<tr><td></td><td>☐</td><td>☐</td><td></td><td></td><td></td></tr>
<tr><td></td><td>☐</td><td>☐</td><td></td><td></td><td></td></tr>
<tr><td></td><td>☐</td><td>☐</td><td></td><td></td><td></td></tr>
<tr><td></td><td>☐</td><td>☐</td><td></td><td></td><td></td></tr>
<tr><td></td><td>☐</td><td>☐</td><td></td><td></td><td></td></tr>
</table>

9.8 Self-actualisation

Self actualisation is about knowing your own strengths and weaknesses, planning how you can improve and setting yourself targets for how you will make the improvements. Self-actualisation for you is, quite simply, doing what is needed to become a customer service professional.

Just by taking part in this programme you are developing yourself as a professional. Here are some other ways of developing your professionalism:

- Gain a Vocationally Related Qualification (VRQ) in customer service
- Go a step further by gaining a Scottish/National Vocational Qualification (S/NVQ) in customer service - you already have the underpinning knowledge - to gain the S/NVQ you will need to show your assessor that you can perform your customer service job to the national standard
- Join a professional organisation - such as the Institute of Customer Service - to access information and ideas to help you perform even better
- Use customer service websites to keep up with the latest ideas
- Read journals and books about customer service
- Observe your colleagues who are effective in delivering service excellence - you can learn a lot from them
- Ask a colleague or a manager to review your performance to identify where you can improve

Complete the following questionnaire to check your own standards as a customer service professional:

Activity

Check your customer service professionalism

		Never	Occasionally	Half the time	Frequently	Always
1	I serve customers courteously and promptly	☐	☐	☐	☐	☐
2	I can answer customer questions about my organisation's products and services	☐	☐	☐	☐	☐
3	I wait for customers to finish speaking before responding	☐	☐	☐	☐	☐
4	I look at a complaining or dissatisfied customer as an opportunity	☐	☐	☐	☐	☐
5	I get personal satisfaction from acting professionally when providing a service to customers	☐	☐	☐	☐	☐
6	I am aware of my body language and the impression I am creating	☐	☐	☐	☐	☐
7	I make sure that my appearance creates a professional image	☐	☐	☐	☐	☐
8	I work co-operatively with all my colleagues and support them in customer service situations	☐	☐	☐	☐	☐
9	I listen to customers with an open mind	☐	☐	☐	☐	☐
10	I choose my words carefully to communicate effectively with customers	☐	☐	☐	☐	☐

At the start of this programme you listed up to three personal objectives. As you worked through the programme you included items in your learning log. For this activity you will refine these items, plus any other aspects that you feel are needed, to produce your Five-Step Improvement Plan. This will be up to five clear steps that you will take in your customer service role to bring about significant improvements for your customers.

Activity

Five-step improvement plan

List the five key steps that you will take to bring about clear benefits for your customers. State what those benefits are, and set yourself a target completion date for each action.

5 steps	Action	Benefits to customers	Target date
Step 1			
Step 2			
Step 3			
Step 4			
Step 5			

193

Educating the customer

Educate your customers! To keep them loyal they need to know all about you. Your organisation, its products and its services may be very new to your customers. It is a difficult job to inform your customers (and potential new customers) about what you have to offer.

Follow these guidelines to educate the customers:

- Use every communication (face-to-face, telephone, email, promotional materials) as a chance to tell your customers about you, your products and services
- Ensure your promotional materials are nothing less than 100% accurate and totally effective at getting the message across
- Tell your customers about your systems – they want to know how to do business with you
- Tell your customers what you have done and what you will do next

Winning more business

Whether you work for a profit-maker or a not-for-profit organisation you can win more business and contribute to the success of the organisation. Every organisation needs success. This success is built on reputation, and to keep that reputation as high as possible the customers need to be delighted.

It is your job as a customer service professional to:

- Provide the best possible standards of service to your customers
- Keep existing customers loyal by meeting and exceeding their expectations
- Present a professional appearance and attitude at all times
- Work with your colleagues and managers to ensure your team functions well for customers
- Be innovative and aware of new opportunities to raise the standards of service
- Constantly look for ways to improve your own and your organisation's performance for customers

By working and improving as a professional you can make a big difference to the success of your organisation.

Winning more business

You now recognise the impact that you individually can have on business success. Give three specific changes that you will introduce or recommend for your organisation to win more business.

1	
2	
3	

195

Make the moment memorable

9.11 Your checklist for service excellence

To keep in mind all the aspects of customer service professionalism, the following checklist will help you when dealing with your customers:

Checklist for service excellence

Greet the customer Customers expect a friendly, positive greeting with eye contact, a smile (if appropriate) and receptive body language.

Determine the customer's needs Finding out what the customer needs tells you how to deal with the rest of the customer interaction. Use your skills of listening and communicating.

Meet the customer's needs Respond effectively by acting quickly and with confidence. Recognise what you must do to deliver the promise to the customer. Try your best to exceed the customer's expectations.

Make the moment memorable This is where you need to be creative and imaginative. Do something special. It could be something big or something little. Whatever it is, it makes the customer feel good.

Check the results You can be the first to get customer feedback very simply by asking a question such as: "How was our service today?" You might ask with sincerity: "Is there anything else I can do for you?" This is a perfect way of checking whether all the customer's needs have been met.

Leave the door open Encourage your customers to return to your organisation. Customers like to be appreciated. You might say: "I hope we can help you again", or simply: "Thanks for your support – hope to see you next time."

9.12 Self-assessment

Module 9 Self-assessment

In each case tick the answer that best fits the question.

1	Self-actualisation includes:	Recognising your own strengths and weaknesses	A	☐
		Planning for promotion	B	☐
		Recovering from illness	C	☐
2	Interrupting other people can be seen as:	Adult behaviour	A	☐
		Submissive behaviour	B	☐
		Aggressive behaviour	C	☐
3	Your personal life can:	Influence your working life	A	☐
		Have no effect of your job performance	B	☐
		Get in the way of your job	C	☐
4	Educating customers is useful because:	They may not be well-qualified	A	☐
		It will help them to complete the paperwork	B	☐
		It helps them understand what you have done and will do next	C	☐
5	You can effectively gain feedback from your customers by saying:	How was our service today?	A	☐
		How can I help you?	B	☐
		Have a nice day	C	☐

197

9.13 Learning log

Now complete your learning log.

Learning log for Module 9

Add items to your learning log. When you get to the end of the programme you will need to refine these items to produce a clear action plan.

What I have learned
1
2
3
4
5

Actions planned	Target date
1	
2	
3	
4	
5	

198

Module summary

- Well done – in this module you have learned about the importance of your own attitude and emotional well-being on the way you deliver customer service. You should now be able to select the right emotional response to customers, particularly in difficult situations. Improving your own skills and knowledge is an important way to develop your job performance and your standard of customer service delivery.

Answers to self-assessments

Module 1 self-assessment: Basic concepts of customer service

1	B	2	B	3	A	4	C	5	B

Module 2 self-assessment: Developing relationships with your customers

1	A	2	B	3	C	4	C	5	A

Module 3 self-assessment: Customer service in types of organisations

1	B	2	C	3	A	4	C	5	A

Module 4 self-assessment: Match features and benefits

1	B	2	C	3	B	4	A	5	B

Module 5 self-assessment: Communicate effectively

1	B	2	B	3	A	4	C	5	B

Module 6 self-assessment: Deliver service excellence through teamwork

1	C	2	B	3	C	4	B	5	A

Module 7 self-assessment: Systems for delivering service excellence

1	B	2	A	3	B	4	A	5	C

Module 8 self-assessment: Laws & codes of practice

1	A	2	C	3	A	4	C	5	C

Module 9 self-assessment: The you factor

1	A	2	C	3	A	4	C	5	A

200

S/NVQ knowledge matrix

This matrix shows the where the knowledge and understanding requirements of the U.K.'s Level 2 NOS for Customer Service are covered in this Best Practice Guide.

S/NVQ Knowledge Matrix

This matrix shows where to find the knowledge items of each S/NVQ Unit in this Best Practice Guide.

Unit 1 Prepare yourself to deliver good customer service

Knowledge item		Section
1a	what the organisation does	3.2 4.2
1b	what services or products the organisation provides	1.7 4.2 4.3
1c	what the key features of the organisation's services or products are	4.3
1d	what the key benefits of the organisation's services or products are	4.3
1e	what the structure of the organisation is	2.4
1f	what a customer is	2.2
1g	who the organisation's customers are	4.3
1h	what building an organisation's reputation means	2.3
1i	what can damage an organisation's reputation	2.5
1j	what customer service is	1.2
1k	how customer satisfaction depends on customer expectations and service delivery	1.4
1l	how customer service affects the success of the organisation	2.6
1m	the key customer service requirements of the job	2.4
1n	how company procedures contribute to consistent and reliable customer service	7.3
1o	the kinds of information the organisation keeps about its customers	8.4

Unit 5 Provide customer service within the rules

Knowledge item		Section
5a	organisational procedures that relate to your job	8.2 8.11
5b	limits of what you are allowed to do	8.2
5c	what might endanger customers or their property	8.7
5d	what health and safety risks and hazards might be faced by your customers	8.7
5e	why it is important to respect customer and organisation confidentiality	8.4
5f	the main regulations that apply to your job	8.2
	the main things you must do and not do in your job under laws covering:	
	• equal opportunities	4.5
	• disability discrimination	8.6
5g	• data protection	8.4
	• health and safety	8.7
	• employment responsibility and rights	8.2
	• consumer protection	8.3
5h	the security arrangements of your organisation and how they apply to your job role	8.7

Unit 9 Give customers a positive impression of yourself and your organisation

Knowledge item		Section
9a	your organisation's standards for appearance and behaviour	5.6 5.8 9.3
9b	your organisation's guidelines for how to recognise what your customer wants and respond appropriately	4.3
9c	your organisation's rules and procedures regarding the methods of communication you use	5.3 5.4 5.9 5.10
9d	how to recognise when a customer is angry or confused	5.4 9.3 9.5
9e	your organisation's standards for timeliness in responding to customer questions and requests for information	1.9 4.4 8.4

Unit 10   Promote additional services or products to customers

Knowledge item		Section
10a	your organisation's procedures and systems for encouraging the use of additional services or products	4.6
10b	how the use of additional services or products will benefit your customers	4.6
10c	how your customer's use of additional services or products will benefit your organisation	4.6
10d	the main factors that influence customers to use your services or products	2.4 4.6
10e	how to introduce additional services or products to customers outlining their benefits, overcoming reservations and agreeing to provide the additional services or products	4.6
10f	how to give appropriate, balanced information to customers about services or products	4.3 4.6

Unit 11   Process customer service information

Knowledge item		Section
11a	your organisation's procedures and guidelines for collecting, retrieving and supplying customer service information	7.11 8.4
11b	how to collect customer service information efficiently and effectively	7.11
11c	how to operate the customer service information storage system	7.11
11d	why processing customer service information correctly makes an important contribution to effective customer service	7.11
11e	the importance of attention to detail when processing customer service information	7.11
11f	legal and regulatory restrictions on the storage of data	8.4

Unit 12   Live up to the customer service promise

Knowledge item		Section
12a	the key features, moments of truth (those points in the customer service process that have the most impact on the customer experience) and customer experiences that define the organisation's service offer, vision and promise	3.2 1.10
12b	ways in which staff can contribute to communicating the service vision or promise to customers	2.4
12c	sales, marketing and/or public relations reasons for defining a service offer, vision and promise	2.4
12d	how words can be used and adapted to reflect a defined service offer, vision and promise	4.4
12e	how actions can be used and adapted to reflect a defined service offer, vision and promise	4.4

Unit 13 Make customer service personal

Knowledge item		Section
13a	how use of your customer's name makes service more personal	2.4 4.6
13b	personality types and their receptiveness to personalised services	5.8 9.3
13c	types of personal information about customers that should and should not be kept on record	8.4
13d	features of personal service that are most appreciated by customers with individual needs	4.5
13e	body language and approaches to communication that are generally interpreted as open	5.5
13f	your organisation's guidelines on actions that are permissible outside of the normal routines and procedures	8.2 8.11
13g	your own preferences and comfort levels relating to how you are willing and able to personalise service	5.8 9.3 9.7

Unit 14 Go the extra mile in customer service

Knowledge item		Section
14a	your organisation's service offer	1.7
14b	how customers form expectations of the service they will receive	1.4
14c	what types of service action most customers will see as adding value to the customer service they have already had	1.7
14d	your organisation's rules and procedures that determine your authority to go the extra mile	8.2 8.11
14e	relevant legislation and regulation that impact on your freedom to go the extra mile	8.2 8.11
14f	how your organisation receives customer service feedback on the types of customer experience that has impressed them	1.9 7.7
14g	your organisation's procedures for making changes in its service offer	7.6

Unit 15 Deal with customers in writing or using ICT

Knowledge item		Section
15a	the importance of using clear and concise language	5.2
15b	the additional significance and potential risks involved in committing a communication to a permanent record format	8.4
15c	the effects of style and tone on the reader of a written or ICT communication	5.10
15d	the importance of adapting your language to meet the needs of customers who may find the communication hard to understand	5.10 7.11 8.6
15e	your organisation's guidelines and procedures relating to written communication and the use of ICT to communicate	5.10 8.4
15f	how to operate equipment used for producing and sending written or ICT communications	7.11
15g	the importance of keeping your customer informed if there is likely to be any delay in responding to a communication	7.8 7.11
15h	the risks associated with the confidentiality of written or ICT communications	8.4

Unit 16 Deal with customers face to face

Knowledge item		Section
16a	the importance of speaking clearly and slowly when dealing with a customer face to face	5.4
16b	the importance of taking the time to listen carefully to what the customer is saying	5.4
16c	your organisation's procedures that impact on the way you are able to deal with your customers face to face	5.4
16d	the features and benefits of your organisation's services or products	4.3
16e	your organisation's service offer and how it affects the way you deal with customers face to face	1.7 5.4
16f	the principles of body language that enable you to interpret customer feelings without verbal communication	5.5
16g	how individual transactions between people can be understood by using a behavioural model such as transactional analysis	5.8
16h	why the expectations and behaviour of individual customers will demand different responses to create rapport and achieve customer satisfaction	5.8
16i	the agreed and recognised sector cues in customer behaviour that indicate that your customer expects a particular action by you	5.4 5.5 5.7 8.11

Unit 17 Deal with customers by telephone

	Knowledge item	Section
17a	the importance of speaking clearly and slowly when dealing with customers by telephone	5.9
17b	the effects of smiling and other facial expressions that can be detected by somebody listening to you on the telephone	5.9
17c	the importance of adapting your speech to meet the needs of customers who may find your language or accent hard to understand	5.9
17d	your organisation's guidelines and procedures for the use of telephone equipment	5.9
17e	your organisation's guidelines and procedures for what should be said during telephone conversations with customers	5.9
17f	what details should be included if taking a message for a colleague	5.9
17g	how to operate the organisation's telephone equipment	5.9
17h	the importance of keeping your customer informed if they are on hold during a call	5.9
17i	the importance of not talking over an open telephone	5.9
17j	your organisation's guidelines for handling abusive calls	5.9

Unit 21 Deliver reliable customer service

	Knowledge item	Section
21a	your organisation's procedures and systems for delivering customer service	8.2 8.11
21b	methods or systems for measuring an organisation's effectiveness in delivering customer service	1.9 7.7
21c	your organisation's procedures and systems for checking service delivery	2.4 7.7
21d	your organisation's requirements for health and safety in your area of work	8.7

Unit 22 Deliver customer service on your customer's premises

	Knowledge item	Section
22a	the importance of sensitivity to people's feelings about their own premises and possessions	8.7
22b	the regulatory and legal restrictions on what you can and cannot do in all aspects of your work	8.2 8.7
22c	the insurance implications of working on your customer's premises	8.7
22d	the organisational procedures you would take if any accidental damage is incurred by you on your customer's premises	8.7

Unit 23 Recognise diversity when delivering customer service

Knowledge item		Section
23a	the importance of recognising diversity in relation to age, disability, national origin, religion, sexual orientation, values, ethnic culture, education, lifestyle, beliefs, physical appearance, social class and economic status	4.5 8.6
23b	reasons why consideration of diversity and inclusion issues affect customer service	4.5
23c	organisational guidelines to make customer service inclusive for diverse groups of customers	4.5 8.6
23d	legal use and meaning of the word 'reasonable'	8.6
23e	how to observe and interpret non-verbal clues	4.5
23f	how to listen actively for clues about your customer's expectations and needs	5.5 5.7
23g	techniques for obtaining additional information from customers through tactful and respectful questions	4.5 5.4 5.7
23h	behaviour that might cause offence to specific groups of people to whom you regularly provide customer service	4.5 8.6
23i	how to impress specific groups of people to whom you regularly provide customer service	4.5 8.6

207

Unit 6 Recognise and deal with customer queries, requests and problems

Knowledge item		Section
6a	who in the organisation is able to give help and information	4.2
6b	limits of what they are allowed to do	8.2 8.11
6c	what professional behaviour is	9.2
6d	how to speak to people who are dissatisfied	5.8 7.9 9.3 9.5
6e	how to deal with difficult people	5.8 7.9
6g	what customers normally expect	1.4 7.4
6h	how to recognise a problem from what a customer says or does	5.7 9.3
6i	what kinds of behaviours/actions would make situations worse	5.8 9.3
6j	the organisational procedures you must follow when you deal with problems or complaints	7.7 7.8
6k	understand the types of behaviour that makes a problem worse	5.8 9.3 9.5

Unit 31   Resolve customer service problems

Knowledge item		Section
31a	organisational procedures and systems for dealing with customer service problems	7.8
31b	how to defuse potentially stressful situations	5.8 7.8 9.5
31c	how to negotiate	5.8 7.8
31d	the limitations of what you can offer your customer	7.8

Unit 36 Develop customer relationships

Knowledge item		Section
36a	the importance of customer retention	2.3 2.5
36b	how your own behaviour affects the behaviour of the customer	5.8
36c	how to behave assertively and professionally at all times	9.5
36d	how to defuse potentially stressful situations	5.8 7.8 9.5
36e	the limitations of the service offer	1.7 3.3
36f	how customer expectations may change as they deal with your organisation	2.5
36g	the cost and resource implications of an extension of the service offer to meet or exceed customer expectations	2.5 4.6
36h	the cost implications of bringing in new customers as opposed to retaining existing customers	2.5
36i	who to refer to when considering any variation to the service offer	4.6 8.2

Unit 37   Support customer service improvements

Knowledge item		Section
37a	how customer experience is influenced by the way service is delivered	1.4 2.5
37b	how customer feedback is obtained	1.9 7.7
37c	how to work with others to identify and support change in the way service is delivered	7.4 7.6 7.7
37d	why it is important to give a positive impression to your customer about the changes made by your organisation even if you disagree with them	5.2 9.6 9.9

Unit 38 Develop personal performance through delivering customer service

Knowledge item		Section
38a	your organisation's systems and procedures for developing personal performance in customer service	9.2
38b	how your behaviour has an effect on the behaviour of others	6.4 9.2
38c	how effective learning depends on a process of planning, doing and reviewing	2.4
38d	how to review effectively your personal strengths and development needs	9.8
38e	how to put together a personal development plan that will build on your strengths and overcome your weaknesses in areas that are important to customer service	Learning logs + 9.8
38f	how to access sources of information and support for your learning	9.8
38g	how to obtain useful and constructive personal feedback from others	6.5 6.6 9.8
38h	how to respond positively to personal feedback	9.2 9.3 9.7 9.8

209

References

Texts

Armistead, C., Beamish, N. and Kiely, J., 2001, *Emerging skills for a changing economy: Evolution of the Customer Service Professional*, Institute of Customer Service.

Barlow, N., 2001, *Batteries Included!: Creating Legendary Service*, Random House Business Books

Berne, E., 2004, *Games People Play: The Psychology of Human Relationships*, Penguin Books Ltd

Codling, S., 1998, *Benchmarking*, Gower

Institute of Customer Service, 2006, *National Occupational Standards in Customer Service 2006*, Institute of Customer Service

Johnston, R., 2001, *Service Excellence = Reputation = Profit*, Institute of Customer Service

Johnston, R., 2003, *Delivering Service Excellence: The View from the Front Line*, Institute of Customer Service

Smith, S. and Wheeler, J., 2002, *Managing the Customer Experience: Turning Customers into Advocates*, Financial Times Prentice Hall

Research reports

ABA Research Ltd and Surrey University, 2003, *Research Report*, ABA Research Ltd

Bain & Co., 1998, *The Future of Customer Service*, Institute of Customer Service

James, G., 2003, *National Complaints Culture Survey 2003*, TMI/Institute of Customer Service

Hicks, C., 2004, *National Complaints Culture Survey 2004*, TMI/Institute of Customer Service

Customer service websites

www.instituteofcustomerservice.com   Institute of Customer Service

www.ecustomerserviceworld.com   E-Customer Service World

www.customerserviceawards.com   Customer Service Awards

www.customer1st.co.uk   Customer 1st International

Index

211